RAF Kit Through the Ages

The Development of Personal Equipment and Flying Gear Worn by RAF Pilots and Aircrew Over the Last Century

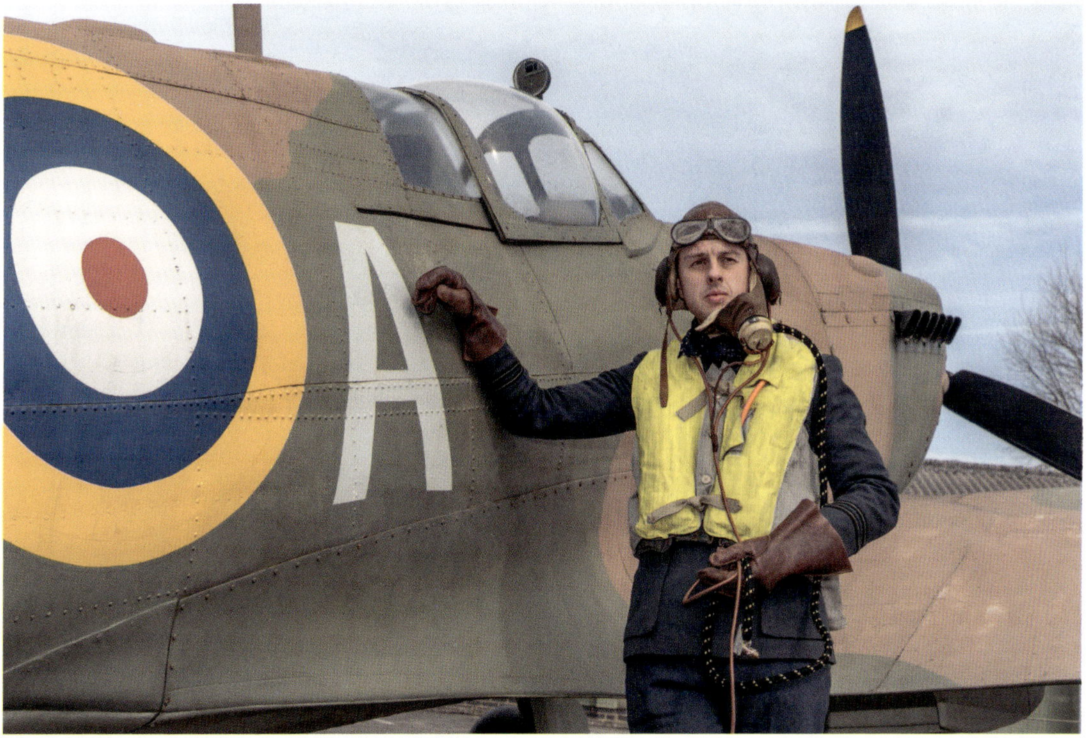

LEE CHAPMAN AND JED JAGGARD

Front cover image: Our member of the RAF airborne early warning team heads out to join the rest of the crew of a Mk 2 Shackleton in the early 1970s.

Back cover image: Our Gloster Meteor pilot from the early post-World War Two period.

Title page image: Our pilot wearing Battle of Britain-era kit next to the Yorkshire Air Museum's replica Spitfire.

Contents page image: Our two Airman greet each other. A member of the RAF aircrew from 1918 shakes hands with a Harrier pilot of the late 1990s.

Published by Key Books
An imprint of Key Publishing Ltd
PO Box 100
Stamford
Lincs PE9 1XQ

www.keypublishing.com

The right of Lee Chapman and Jed Jaggard to be identified as the authors of this book has been asserted in accordance with the Copyright, Designs and Patents Act 1988 Sections 77 and 78.

Copyright © Lee Chapman and Jed Jaggard, 2023

ISBN 978 1 80282 480 3

All rights reserved. Reproduction in whole or in part in any form whatsoever or by any means is strictly prohibited without the prior permission of the Publisher.

Typeset by SJmagic DESIGN SERVICES, India.

Contents

Foreword 4
Acknowledgements 5
Introduction 6
Chapter 1   World War One Pilots' Kit 10
Chapter 2   RAF Pilots' Kit During the Interwar Years (1918–38) 21
Chapter 3   RAF Pilots' Kit During World War Two; Part 1 (1939–42) 31
Chapter 4   RAF Pilots' Kit During World War Two; Part 2 (1943–45) 39
Chapter 5   Post-World War Two Pilots' Kit (1945–52) 46
Chapter 6   RAF Second Generation Jet Pilot Kit (1952–59) 53
Chapter 7   RAF Third Generation Jet Pilot Kit (1960–69) 61
Chapter 8   RAF Pilots' Kit During the 1970s 68
Chapter 9   RAF Pilots' Kit During the 1980s and the Falklands War 74
Chapter 10   RAF Pilots' Kit During the 1990s and the Gulf War 83
Chapter 11   Contemporary RAF Pilots' Kit 89
Summary 95

Foreword

Co-author Jed Jaggard is one of the UK's most enthusiastic historical reenactors and curates a vast collection of RAF Kit covering all periods of its history. The images featured in this book have all been taken by Jed's co-author, Lee Chapman, and feature Jed (and occasionally a few friends) demonstrating the kit in authentically recreated scenes designed to bring the history to life. The kit collections represented in this book are all fully researched and based on period documents and photographs, cross-referenced wherever possible. However, readers should note that the use of specific kit in any period of history was far from standardised, and many pilots would modify their own kit or hang on to outdated equipment well-beyond its official usage. This would be exacerbated during wartime when aircraft and weaponry updates would accelerate at a rate that kit designers and distributors could not always match. Therefore, the representations in this book show typical examples used at significant moments in RAF history, but the authors acknowledge that those illustrated may be one of many variations. The book provides an introduction to this fascinating subject, and since it does not aim to cover every item of kit used in the RAF's history, it instead focuses on significant changes and developments at crucial moments. Finally, readers should note that this book focuses on fixed-wing frontline aircraft. The authors acknowledge that there is much more to talk about in rotary and training aircraft and hope to address this in future publications.

For further information please see www.chappersphotography.co.uk and www.upanatemhistory.co.uk

Our pilot demonstrates the kit typically worn by early Panavia Tornado pilots. He stands next to the Yorkshire Air Museum's Tornado.

Acknowledgements

The author and publisher would like to thank the Yorkshire Air Museum for permissions to photograph the exhibits on its sites. For additional imagery, the authors also want to thank Coventry Airport, Wellesbourne Mountford Airfield, RNAS Yeovilton, East Midlands Aeropark, the Imperial War Museums, Stow Maries Great War Aerodrome and the Royal Air Force Museum. Every attempt has been made to seek permissions for copyright material and photographic rights. However, if we have inadvertently used materials without permission, we apologise, and we will make the necessary correction at the first opportunity.

Lee Chapman would also like to thank his close family for continual motivation, support and encouragement. He would also like to thank Ian at Airscene for offering fantastic opportunities to get up close to aircraft, and Andy Forester and Dan Gooch for joining him on many photography missions near and far. He would also like to thank co-author Jed for curating a fine collection of kit and also for his patience when posing for many, many photographs. Finally, Lee would also like to acknowledge the support from the team at the Yorkshire Air Museum in allowing access to a unique collection of aircraft for the images created for this book.

Jed Jaggard would like to thank several people without whom this collecting obsession, and consequently this book, would not have been possible: Robin Pettifer, whose hospitality and kit-rummaging over tea have given him access to a range of variations of equipment; Gary Hancock, whose knowledge of all things RAF equipment-related, from aircraft to survival and from clothing to kit, has been a constant mine of information over the years; and Lee Chapman, who thought this book was possible! To all the museums, groups and trusts and their volunteers and staff who work tirelessly to restore and present the fabulous aircraft in this book, it is a great privilege to be able to get hands-on with their incredible hard work. Jed would also like to thank his parents, who initially allowed him to have all the kit strewn over the house in his early years of collecting, and finally to his wife, Jess, who has now taken on this mantle! She is a source of constant support for all the historical things he undertakes, and without which none of his working life would be possible.

Our airman and officer of the newly formed RAF discuss work to be done, somewhere in France, in 1918.

Introduction

This book illustrates the history of the RAF's pilot and aircrew kit, exploring how the personal equipment and flying gear issued to service personnel has changed throughout time.

Innovations in kit and personal equipment have evolved to keep pace with the ever-improving technology and performance of aircraft, and over the last 100 years, aviation has gone through some considerable changes. As aircraft designs improved, so too did the kit used by pilots and crew.

From the first days of powered-flight, pilots have required protection against the elements. Initially, a nice warm jacket, a pair of goggles and a hat were sufficient to protect the aviator who, although exposed to extremes of air temperature, would travel close to the ground at slow speeds. As the performance of aircraft designs progressed, aeroplanes could fly faster, higher and for longer. Therefore, the need for purpose-designed clothing and kit became essential for the pilot's own safety.

For every 1,000ft climbed, air temperature typically drops by around 2°C. By the end of World War One, aircraft were regularly reaching 19,000ft, which means the air temperature could easily be below -20°C on a summer's day. Early aircraft had open cockpits and no heating systems, leaving pilots exposed to the brutal elements. The insulated clothing issued to pilots and observers was truly lifesaving.

The Gloster Gladiator was the first RAF fighter aircraft with an enclosed cockpit, but this did not

The Gloster Gladiator was the first RAF fighter with an enclosed cockpit.

arrive until the mid-1930s. The advent of the enclosed cockpit and eventually heated cockpit mitigated the need for warmer clothing, but increases in aircraft performance meant pilots were subject to higher g forces, speeds, and lower air pressure, which created other requirements such as the need for oxygen masks. Innovations in kit designs ensure that pilots were able to withstand the rigours of high-performance flying. As flight technology developed, the kit became safer, more durable, and better connected to the aircraft.

These are far from the only hazards that powered flight could inflict on the relativity frail human body; open-cockpit aviators were subject to a phenomenon known as air-blast when travelling at high speeds; they are also subject to deafening noises and extreme heat from engines, machinery, and weapons. Additionally, toxic substances from engine exhausts coupled with low-oxygen levels at altitude could be suffocating. During wartime, pilots can also be threatened by the effects of fire, oil spills, bright lights, impacts and the potential effects of chemical, biological, and even nuclear weapons. A fully equipped pilot must also be ready to safely leave their aircraft mid-flight in an emergency, fully prepared for the possibility of landing in a remote or hostile location such as a desert or a freezing cold ocean.

The Battle of Britain-era pilot would always fly equipped with a parachute ready to bail out, a luxury not offered to the pilots of World War One.

Above: Our pilot in basic World War One gear, about to climb into an SE5a.

Left: Our pilot wearing the modern kit used in the Eurofighter Typhoon, a world away from the kit used over 100 years ago when the RAF was formed.

Personal protection is not the only goal of a pilot's kit. Once suitably protected, a pilot must still be able to operate the aircraft and weapons, think clearly, communicate, calculate, navigate and monitor their surroundings at all times. Many, often-unsung, great minds have found solutions to these problems that are just as innovative and fascinating as the aircraft in which the pilot flies. As the demands of flight are completely different in modern times, it is no surprise that the kit used by today's RAF pilots differs dramatically from the kit used when the RAF was formed in 1918.

This book tells the story of RAF kit development using brand new images of original and authentic replica kit as worn by RAF aircrew throughout history. The images will feature detailed studies of the kit in isolation as well as images that place the kit in the correct historical context, including authentic re-enactments using aircraft of the period.

Our two pilots discuss their aerial exploits after a recent scramble.

Chapter 1
World War One Pilots' Kit

World War One took place just after the birth of powered flight, when aerial technology was still in its infancy. At the outbreak of war, the military potential of this novelty invention was not fully recognised. However, some forward-thinking Entente (Allied) commanders soon realised the advantages of using the aeroplane to see what the enemy was planning on the other side of the hill.

Two late World War One pilots discuss flight plans ahead of an operation.

At the start of World War One, the Royal Flying Corp (RFC) took just four squadrons of primitive aircraft to France. In 1914, their only purpose was to gain information. Pilots soon found that they would have to fight for this information and so began the first, crude duels in the air. As the fighting intensified, a technological war began to run parallel to the one above the trenches. The need for ever-more sophisticated aircraft grew as each side developed their own purpose-built fighters, known as scouts. The potential military purposes of ever-improving aircraft designs soon became apparent to both sides, and by 1918 there were different flying machines specifically built for bombing, day-fighting, night-fighting, escorting and reconnaissance.

Although the RFC and Royal Naval Air Service (RNAS) had valiantly defended Britain, provided vital army reconnaissance, and taken the fight to Germany, it soon became clear that a more centrally organised approach to air warfare was required. Increasingly devastating German attacks on London prompted a review into British air power. Lt Gen Jan Smuts was commissioned to conduct a review, and in his six-page report known as the Smuts Report, he recommended the formation of an independent air force on par in status with the British Army and Royal Navy.

Smuts suggested that the RFC and RNAS be amalgamated into the Royal Air Force (RAF). Prime Minister David Lloyd George concurred, and the RAF was officially formed on 1 April 1918. Britain was the first nation in the world to form its own stand-alone air force, which on its formation was

Our late World War One pilot prepares to board the Yorkshire Air Museum's replica Royal Aircraft Factory SE5a as it runs up its engine.

equipped with 20,000 aircraft and over 300,000 men, the largest air force in the world at that time. It was far cry from the four squadrons of ramshackle aircraft that plodded their way across the English Channel four years earlier.

Despite the RAF being a new force, it initially relied on aircraft inherited from the RFC and RNAS, which included many aircraft that had long been out-dated by technological advancements. Aircraft such as the Sopwith Pup had been in service since 1916, and two years of war had seen rapid developments in aviation. Newer models such as the Royal Aircraft Factory SE5a, were more capable but not available in the numbers required. The same can be said for the kit worn by its pilots, and there would be no sudden influx of newly developed kit for the world's first air force.

The final stages of World War One saw a slow transition of flying gear and equipment from the British Army-controlled days of the RFC as it merged with the RNAS to form the RAF.

In the picture below, the subject wears very similar clothing to that worn by pilots at to the outbreak of war in 1914, the only thing to betray the dates is a late war-produced Royal Aircraft Factory SE5a biplane. As a commissioned officer, in this case a Second Lieutenant, he wears brown boots. He has a pair of light-brown whipcord breeches that came in a variety of shades and designs. As an officer, he would be expected to purchase his own equipment.

The jacket is the 'maternity jacket' introduced for other ranks in 1912, and although it was being worn by some officers the same year, it was not given official approval until 1913. Fastened

Our late World War One pilot stands in front of Yorkshire Air Museum's replica Royal Aircraft Factory SE5a.

with concealed buttons and hooks, for aircrew their insignia was displayed on their left breast with either wings for pilots or a half-wing (known as a brevet) with a large 'O' for observer. It had pockets either side and was worn with a Sam Browne belt, which had been in use with the army since the 1800s. Rank was displayed on the epaulettes, and collar badges (known as 'collar dogs' on formal uniforms) were worn with the letters 'RFC' surrounded by a wreath surmounted by a crown.

Our pilot wears a side cap, although some pictures from the time show pilots wearing a standard officer peaked cap. This has a bronze cap badge like the one on the collar but slightly larger. The material is a fine woollen cloth mixed with silk or cotton known as baratea, rather than the rough serge fabric issued to the other ranks.

Studying a map before his next sortie, in the image below, our subject has begun to don some flying gear. Although there were approved styles of dress and later formal regulations of pattern, many airmen purchased their own leather coats in the early stages of the war. Often worn with a liner, leather coats provided good protection against the cold and the risk of fire. Our pilot is also wearing thick, long socks and shoes for this mission, with a white silk scarf around his neck for warmth.

Over his coat is an early life preserver, manufactured by the company Boddy. This design is the No. 5. Available for purchase since 1910, life preservers had been considered by the RFC in 1913 but were initially rejected. The No. 5 was officially adopted in 1916, although its use was restricted to aircrew below 5ft 9in. Presumably anyone over this height was tall enough to reach the bottom of the English Channel!

Very few men had experience of flying in 1914, and so pilots were often chosen for their skills on a horse or a sailing boat in hope that skills of balance and proprioception would transfer to aircraft handling. The aircraft they flew were primitive and required

Our pilot studies the map for the next mission. He is wearing an early form of life preserver at the RAF Museum in Cosford.

A closer view of the early life preserver.

constant management in the air, and they were built of light weight, flimsy, flammable materials that could fail at any time. Pilots of World War One were not issued with a parachute, as it was thought to inspire cowardice, but many did carry a revolver. This small handgun was little use against the enemy in the skies, but many doomed pilots would consider using one to bring about a quick end when faced with an uncontrollable aircraft fire or thought of a long fall to their death.

The two subjects in the photograph at the bottom of page 15 demonstrate two methods of keeping warm in the air. On the right, the aircrew member is attired in an approved-pattern long version of the leather flying coat with a map pocket on the front. Under this would be the standard uniform. Over his legs are 'Fug' boots. This type of footwear was invented by Maj Hawker VC, DSO, in 1916. His first pair were made at Harrods in London. They are of thigh length with a fleece lining and a suede covering, with buckles and straps to tighten them around the leg. They had a rubber sole and usually a leather toe cap. There are several variations on this design. Occasionally, they were cut down to just below the knee.

To his left the second aircrew member is wearing a fleece-lined flying suit with fur collar known as a 'Sidcot' after its designer, Sidney Cotton. Cotton was a pilot with 8 Squadron RNAS during World War One. On one occasion, he was scrambled quickly without having time to don his flying gear. He was wearing an oil- and grease-soaked overall, which he found helped to retain his body heat. He incorporated this into his own flying suit design. The Sidcot suit quickly became the standard RAF issue, and by 1922 the leather coat and trousers were completely removed from the RAF inventory. The first basic Sidcot suit was continually improved and soon included fireproofing as well as heat insulation.

Evidently describing many of his daring aerial exploits, our main subject has now put his gloves and flying helmet on. His goggles are the early war style, made from red rubber fastened with a two-part strap. The pilot's need for good sight and clear vision cannot be understated, and even from the early days, the use of goggles for protection against air-blast was standard. During World War One, the Mk I and Mk II goggles were issued by the RFC. The Mk I had a clear Triplex lens, while the Mk II was tinted. By 1933, the Mk III goggles became standard issue, but these featured a curved plastic lens that caused some distortion of vision, and as such the Mk II goggles were retained by some pilots into World War Two.

Key Publishing Limited
Customer Services
P.O.BOX 300
Stamford
Lincolnshire
PE9 1NA
United Kingdom

TELEPHONE: +44 (0) 1780 480404
EMAIL: orders@keypublishing.com
WEBSITE: www.shop.keypublishing.com

Delivery Note

Order Created: 27/02/2023
Order printed:
Date 27/02/2023
Time 13:52:29

2nd Class

SH48834

Deliver To:

F Budd
2 Haselfoot
Letchworth Garden City
ENG
SG6 4DE
United Kingdom

Item Code	Description	Location	Qty
SPECSTEPSPIT	Spitfire Mk.IX (Building the Airfix 1/24 Superkit)	6R-4-D	1
KB0174	Avro Vulcan B.Mk2: A Place in History, 1960–84	SS-1	1
	RAF Kit Through the Ages		1

Thank you for shopping with Key Publishing Ltd.
Please visit our website at shop.keypublishing.com

VAT NO: GB445 5583 29

World War One Pilots' Kit

At the RAF Museum in Cosford, our World War One pilot looks a little more flight-ready with flying helmet and gloves.

The dawn patrol is briefed for take-off sometime in 1917. Two pilots showing alternate methods for keeping warm once aloft. This image was taken at Stow Maries First World War Aerodrome in Essex, in front of a replica Royal Aircraft Factory BE2c.

A closer view of the 'Sidcot' flying suit as our pilot plots his course.

Standing next to an airworthy BE2c, our pilot looks warm and comfortable in his Sidcot suit.

World War One Pilots' Kit

An original World War One sidcot suit, on display at the RAF Museum in Hendon.

Our pilot checking his revolver.

A World War One life preserver on display at the RAF Museum in Hendon.

The helmet (an Mk 1, 22c/12) in the first image on page 15 is one of many styles employed by the RFC. It is like the Mk 1 design but without the leather wind deflectors at the front of the ear flaps. The style of the Mk 1 was introduced around 1916 but was listed by the RAF in 1918 as Flying Helmet, Mk 1, 22c/12.

The gauntlets are, again, one of many designs in use. These are covered in fur with leather on the inside for better grip. He would probably be wearing more / several thinner pairs of gloves underneath.

Above: An original World War One pilot headgear on display at the RAF Museum in Cosford.

Right: The RAF Museum in Hendon houses an excellent collection of World War One flying clothing, including this helmet and goggles on display.

A lieutenant of the RAF (left) stands proudly by his aircraft (a Sopwith 1½ Strutter) in 1918. Officially around for a little over a year, the 1918 pattern uniform and regulations were short lived, as the RAF sort to blend the RNAS and the RFC. Buttons were of RNAS type with gilt metal, with a bird surmounted by crown and surrounded by a rope-type edge. The lace on the sleeves is similar to the Royal Navy jacket but with a sky-blue stripe in the middle. Caps were khaki with a black mohair band and patent-leather peak with chin strap. A system of gold-coloured bars were initially used to help denote rank on either side of the crown but these were soon dropped. Due to shortages, the all-metal Warrant Officer-type badges were used by some officers. The shirt was brown and worn with a black, naval-style tie.

World War One pilots were brave beyond measure. Kit designed during this period was largely about protection from the elements with safety measures often an after-thought. In the early days of powered flight, flying was already a hazardous business even without being shot at, but with inadequate kit it must have been a truly uncomfortable experience too.

Out pilot, now a lieutenant of the RAF, standing next to the RAF Museum Cosford's Sopwith 1½ Strutter.

Chapter 2

RAF Pilots' Kit During the Interwar Years (1918–38)

Following four years of war, the world's population were keen to move on as soon as peace was finally declared on 11 November 1918. Demobilisation was fast; men and women were soon thrown back into their civilian lives. The war was fought at great costs to both sides, and the losses could be measured economically and also in the tragic, unprecedented loss of human lives. While aviation had proven itself as a key asset in waging war, most people felt the need to focus on peace, and so began a rapid disarmament.

When the British military was scaled back in 1919, the RAF was particularly hard hit and had to fight for its own survival. It was reduced to just 35,000 individuals, including 6,500 permanently commissioned officers. Meanwhile, civil aviation began to take-off. It was a slow start initially, as surplus, hastily adapted military aircraft were used, but eventually the commercial and recreational use of aircraft became widespread and more innovative designs appeared. Pilots were focused on ever-more daring feats and sought out records to break in speed, altitude, endurance and distance. This period is often referred to as the Golden Age of Aviation. While civil aviation began to thrive, the RAF clung on to its open cockpit biplanes and changes to pilots' kit were minimal.

Standing by the cockpit of a Gloster Gladiator (page 22), a pilot waits to climb aboard for his next flight. He is wearing a 'Prestige'-style flying suit from the 1930s. The Prestige suit is synonymous with pilots from the Battle of Britain as well as from the pre-World War Two period. These white overalls are commonplace in period photographs from this period and were a popular choice with pilots. Black overalls were also accepted for wear by the Air Ministry, and occasionally navy blue overalls as well, however, the white version is by far the most common. The suit is of one-piece construction and is made from

Our late-1930s pilot in full flying gear.

Our pilot wears the Prestige flying suit.

cotton drill. Removable epaulettes are fitted to the shoulder and fasten with shank buttons, which are held in place with split rings. Pleated patch pockets are located on the chest. The waist belt features a metal buckle. There are many variations on a theme, with different period photographs showing slightly different styles. Most suits were privately purchased and, as such, were tailored differently. Some had zipped cuffs rather than the buttoned ones worn here. Open-topped leg pockets were common and used for storing essential documents such as maps. This was also seen on the Sidcot flying suit.

Above, below and overleaf: **Next to the Hawker Hart, our pilot wears the Prestige flying.**

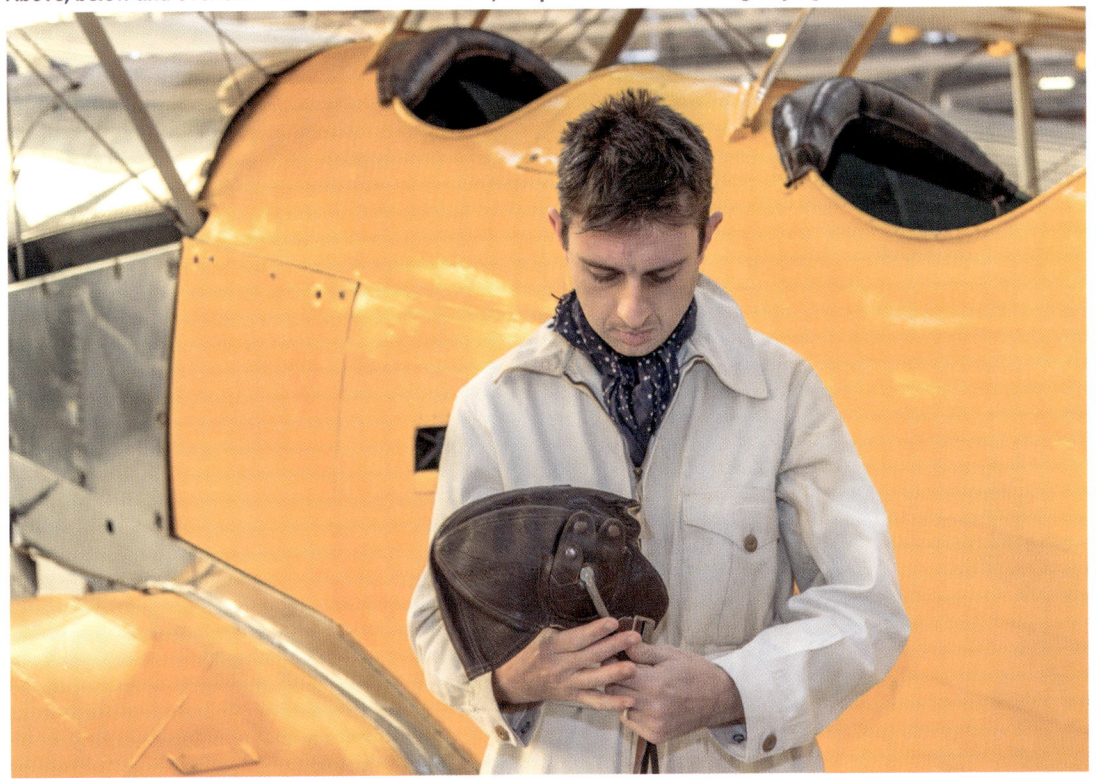

Standing by the cockpit of a Hawker Hart, the pilot is about to go on a training flight. In addition to the Prestige flying suit this interwar pilot wears a pair of fleeced-lined boots, which were like the 1936 pattern boots but without the front 'V' cut out. These were also produced at Harrods.

Above and right: Harrods-made boots.

The pilot is also wearing a leather flying helmet similar to those produced by D. Lewis – Motor Racing, Flying and Aviation Equipment (better known as Lewis Leathers). D. Lewis had premises on Portland Street and Oxford Street in London. This example is made by Aviakit. This style of helmet was popular with the RAF as well as with civilian flyers during this period. The pilot is wearing Gosport tubes in his flying helmet, which would be required in two-seater aircraft to allow for the pilot to communicate with the other members of crew. This set is made from Bakelite and is stamped by the Air Ministry. Gosport tubes work in a similar way to a stethoscope: the earpieces would fix into the ear cups on a flying helmet and the tube from the bottom would fix into the speaking tube of the other crew member.

In the period between the signing of the Treaty of Versailles (28 June 1919) and the beginning of World War Two, the RAF saw little conflict-based action. There were some notable exceptions, for example, in 1920, the RAF helped to bring a conclusion to the long-running Dervish War in Somalia. The RAF's DH9 bombers were used there for bombing campaigns against the religious and military leader Mohammed Abdullah Hassan, the 'Mad Mullah'. The RAF also helped to crush a 1925 rebellion in Waziristan, India, in a conflict that became known as Pink's War, after Wg Cdr R.C.M. Pink who led the three RAF squadrons into battle. After a brief bombing and strafing campaign, the rebel leaders sought out an honourable peace and the war was quickly over.

Most of the RAF's active operations during the interwar period were in hot, dry, and sunny climates. It is therefore no surprise that the kit of this period was influenced by these conditions. The RAF was regarded as the most economical option to police the wide-open spaces across Mesopotamia and the quickest option in the mountain passes of the North West Frontier. A small squadron of aircraft could cover a much larger area than a larger ground force. Kit manufacturers had to provide clothing in suitable camouflage colours and provide adequate protection from the elements.

Gosport tubes were essential tools of communication between two crew members.

Our pilot prepares to board a transport aeroplane about to depart to the Middle East.

Our pilot's kit is neatly packed ready for the journey.

Left and below: An 'ordinary airman' stands beside a Hawker Hart in suitable tropical attire in the late 1930s.

This airman wears the Wolseley-style pith helmet, which had undergone various minor changes since it was introduced in the late 1890s for officers, before becoming standard for all troops prior to the outbreak of World War One. His tunic is uniquely RAF; the tropical version of the blue serge 1919 pattern, these tunics were gradually replaced from the end of the 1930s, with the new pattern and the tailored open collar being introduced from 1936. It has a five-buttoned front with two bottom internal pockets with flaps and two pleated breast pockets with buttoned flaps. The belt was altered to the two-pronged design from the original buttoned style when the jacket underwent changes.

In hot climates, pilots would often wrap light cloth around their necks to prevent sunburn as the sun shone relentlessly on them in their open, exposed cockpit. To mitigate against this, the RAF supplied a new helmet that became known as the Type A. This was specifically for use 'east of Malta' and comprised the body of the traditional pith helmet, complete with brim and ear flaps, and was secured under the chin. It was constructed of lightweight cork and covered with a light khaki drill fabric. Although it provided adequate protection from the sun, it was limited in use due to the drag created by the higher speeds achieved in newer open cockpit aircraft designs.

Although many aircraft companies were competing to produce military aircraft for the RAF during the 1920s and 1930s, there was one that dominated the market above all others. Hawker aircraft were so common during this period that the RAF were often mockingly nicknamed the 'Hawker Air Force'. When the Sopwith company was forced to cease trading at the end of World War One due to excessive war profit taxes, the new Hawker Aircraft company emerged from the ashes. Although some early success was achieved, it was not until Sydney Camm became the chief designer in 1925 that the company really took off.

In 1926, the Air Ministry issued a new specification for a two-seater bomber capable of 160mph, powered by the new Rolls-Royce engine that would eventually be named the Kestrel. Sydney Camm developed the Hawker Hart in response to this ministry request. For its time, it was a ground-breaking aircraft that was 24mph faster than the required specification. With the new Rolls-Royce engine, Camm could fit an aerodynamic cowling around the front of the aircraft, which gave it its sleek look and improved performance. Some Hart's were still in service at the beginning of World War Two as advanced trainers. Famous author and fighter pilot Roald Dahl would conduct his initial training on the Hawker Hart in Iraq. There are two original Harts currently on display in the UK, one at each of the RAF museum sites. K4872 (pictured below) is currently on display at the RAF Museum, Cosford. It was built in 1935 and served with several flight training schools during the build up to World War Two.

The period of peace was short lived, however, and throughout the 1930s the clouds of war began to loom once again. In response, Britain began to scale up its airpower and a new wave of military aircraft designs emerged. During the first part of the decade, the RAF boasted an array of beautiful silver biplanes, which soon

The Type A flying helmet, on display at the RAF Museum, Hendon.

gave way to more sleek monoplane fighters and twin-engine medium-range bombers ready for the imminent war in Europe.

The Gloster SS 37 (Gladiator) prototype was first tested at Martlesham Heath in July 1935, and it reached speeds over 250mph, which was 40mph faster than the current RAF fighter planes. However, it was made obsolete by 30 October that year, when the Hawker Hurricane made its maiden flight and exceeded the Gladiator's top speed by 50mph. Despite this, the Gloster Gladiator still went into service as a stopgap while production was set-up for the new monoplane fighters. The Gladiator features a metal frame, powerful Bristol mercury radial engine and, for the first time on an RAF biplane, an enclosed cockpit. From now on, RAF fighter pilots would have some relief from the elements, but the advancement of aircraft would create new challenges for kit designers.

A Gloster Gladiator and Hawker Hurricane in formation, showing how quickly aircraft designs were changing – the pilots' kit would need to adapt with these developments.

Chapter 3
RAF Pilots' Kit During World War Two; Part 1 (1939–42)

Political tension developed across Europe throughout the 1930s, and it soon became apparent that another war was on the horizon. The promises of peace proved to be short-lived, and whilst most nations had been following a policy of disarmament, it soon became clear that Germany was rapidly re-arming. The British government was forced to look at its home defences, and, given the changes in technology since 1918, it was now likely that the next war would be fought in the air in a more significant way than in World War One. It was clear that Britain's air defences in the mid-1930s were not up to the task of defending the country from invasion and so began a period of expansion that would continue well into the early parts of World War Two.

Somewhere in Northern Ireland, our aircrew discuss their next mission with their Fairy Battle, while on coastal patrol duties in 1941.

At the beginning of World War Two, little had changed in an aircrew's kit compared to the interwar years. Aircraft, including bombers and fighters, were changing to closed cockpits and therefore providing greater protection from air-blast. However, cockpit heating remained glaringly absent, and aircrew continued to suffer from exposure to the low temperatures at altitude. Oxygen masks and systems still failed from the same freezing problems that had happened in the World War One, particularly in the longer-range aircraft.

Although fighter pilots during the early stages of World War Two flew a wide range of aircraft, the iconic Spitfire captures the spirit of the time unlike any other aircraft. The Spitfire was developed by R. J. Mitchell and the team at Supermarine, using their success with a series of racing seaplanes as a starting point. The first flight took place in 1936, just four months after the Hurricane, but delays in early production meant that it was not available in the same numbers when World War Two broke out. Very early Mk I Spitfires were built with a two-bladed fixed-pitch propeller, which was quickly upgraded to a three-blade de Havilland two-pitch version for later production models. Early Spitfires experienced issues with the Merlin II engine and were also uprated to the Merlin III early on. The early Spitfires were capable of up to 367mph and had a range of around 300 miles. The Mk Ia was armed with eight 0.303in Browning machine guns, and experiments took place with cannon-armed Spitfires during the early phases of the war, but they were not operational until much later.

Standing next to a Spitfire (see page 33), a pilot from the early stages of World War Two wears standard flying equipment for 1939. The uniform is the officers' service dress, which hadn't altered greatly since its introduction in 1919. Obscuring his rank are a pair of leather flying gauntlets of pre-war design without a zip. His life preserver is the 1932 pattern produced in a green/grey cloth. This provided problems with identification if pilots had to bail out into the sea, and so they were frequently

Our pilot is now ready to defend his country as the Battle of Britain is about to begin. He stands next to his newly arrived Supermarine Spitfire. This example at the RAF Museum Cosford is the oldest surviving Spitfire.

Our early World War Two pilot stands next to the replica Spitfire at the Yorkshire Air Museum.

painted yellow during the Battle of Britain period to aid rescue boats and aircraft on the search for them. The life preserver contains kapok, a buoyant material, as well as a stole. There is an orange inflation tube on his left-hand side.

On his head is the B-type flying helmet with press stud attachments for the D-type oxygen mask. Oxygen masks had been around in World War One but had only seen limited service in the conflict and interwar period. With the introduction in the 1930s of higher-performance aircraft such as the Spitfire and Hurricane, which could now fly higher, they became a necessity. The mask itself is made from a khaki-coloured fabric with a shammy cover for the microphone. From the side of the microphone is a black and yellow tube that connects into his oxygen supply. The brown cord that goes into the microphone and extends to the flying helmet contains the electronics for his headphones as well as the microphone. Like World War One pilots, he wears goggles made by Triplex, which was now very experienced in the production of aviation eye protection.

Shown on page 35, waiting for another test flight, the pilot has now moved on slightly to the summer of 1940 – the Battle of Britain. The flying helmet, oxygen mask and gloves remain the same, but he has painted his life preserver to make himself more visible should a rescue be required. We can also see his flying boots, which are the fleece-lined boots of 1936 pattern. He wears a thick pair of white woollen socks.

The Battle of Britain is considered by many to be the RAF's finest hour. During the summer of 1940, following the fall of France, Adolf Hitler turned his attentions towards Britain. He knew that a full-scale invasion could only take place if the Luftwaffe had control over the skies. Fortunately, British air defences held firm, and following a summer of frantic, desperate aerial battles, Hitler postponed

A closer view of our early World War Two pilot.

Here our early World War Two pilot stands next to a replica Hawker Hurricane, looking a little less flight ready.

Battle of Britain-era pilot with painted life preserver.

the invasion indefinitely. At the centre of this battle was a small number of RAF pilots that became known as the 'few'; many of the pilots were foreign exiles from Europe or volunteers from Canada and America, and, as such, kit had many personal variations.

To the right of the pilot in the image above is a seat-type parachute with a Canadian pack. During the war, these normally remained in the cockpit waiting for fighter pilots to get in to speed the process up if they were scrambled. As the names suggests, a pilot would sit on the pack once in the aircraft. Aircraft such as the Spitfire had bucket seats to allow the parachute pack to fit in. Between the pack and the pilot was a container for either a dinghy or a cushion depending on the mission. If the planned sortie was likely to take place over sea, then a dinghy would be the preferred option.

Around his waist is a 1937 pattern webbing belt holding a revolver holster and an ammunition pouch. Fighter pilots on combat missions carried a .38 revolver produced by Enfield or Webley for personal protection.

He has a very useful cravat to not only help with the colder temperatures and altitude but to also prevent a sore neck from scanning the skies for the enemy. The designs were down to the individual's taste and could be rather flamboyant! On his head is the standard RAF officers' cap with cloth-covered peak introduced in 1919.

By the autumn of 1940, the day-time dogfights of the Battle of Britain had ceased, but the Luftwaffe continued the night-time bombing of Britain at pace. This created an additional need for night-fighters to protect the major cities from attack. With lack of specifically designed aircraft, the RAF turned to

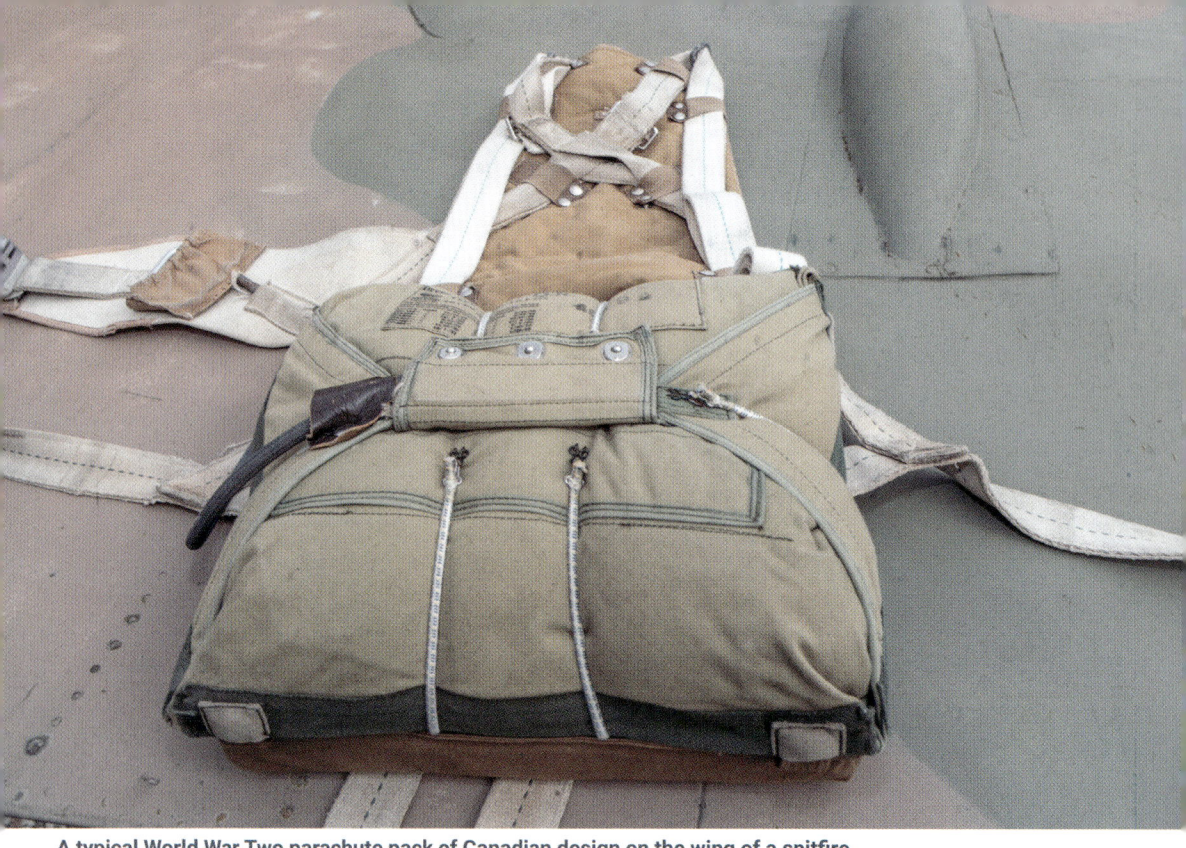

A typical World War Two parachute pack of Canadian design on the wing of a spitfire.

The belt and revolver are just visible in this image.

the surplus types of aircraft to fill the gap. The Boulton Paul Defiant was designed as a day-fighting turret aircraft, but despite some success in the Battle for France, it had proved vulnerable in the Battle of Britain. As a night-fighter it proved itself, but the small escape exists within the turret created an issue for bailing out with a parachute. To combat this, a special parachute-suit was designed by GQ Parachutes. This became known as the 'Parasuit', but it was also sometimes referred to as the 'rhino suit'. The Parasuit integrated a harness and parachute into a single torso-covering garment, which was small and compact enough to allow escape.

The early stages of World War Two were a steep learning curve for the RAF's Fighter Command, and during the Battle of Britain approximately one out of every six pilots were killed in action. Once again, the courage of a small number of brave airmen saved the country from almost certain invasion, but the war would sadly continue. The aircraft manufacturers and kit designers were working hard to give pilots a much-needed edge over the enemy. By the end of World War Two, the much-improved Spitfire could fly twice as high and almost twice as fast. As such, the first half of World War Two drove several rapid changes to the fighter pilot's kit.

The GQ Parasuit was specifically designed for a smooth emergency exit from the small exit space of the Boulton Paul Defiant turret.

The narrow turret of the Boulton Paul Defiant, on display at the RAF Museum Midlands in Cosford.

The famous cravat is clearly visible in this image; our pilot takes a moment out to reflect on the losses of his colleagues during the Battle of Britain.

Chapter 4

RAF Pilots' Kit During World War Two; Part 2 (1943–45)

Whilst the RAF fighter pilots protected the skies over Britain, it was left to the bomber crews to take the battle to the enemy. Bomber Command would fly missions deep into Germany, and these would be long missions, in cramped, cold environments, and were mostly flown at night. At the beginning of the war, the RAF relied on smaller, two-engine bombers like the Vickers Wellington, but towards the end of 1940, larger four-engine bombers began to enter service. The Handley Page Halifax took its first flight in 1939 and entered RAF service in November the following year. It was one of three large British bombers used by the RAF. The bomber was initially powered by four Rolls-Royce Merlin engines, but later models were more commonly given Bristol Hercules powerplants. The heavy bomber performed well for the RAF throughout the war but was generally considered inferior to the Lancaster due to a more limited bomb bay. As such, it was widely used for other duties including as a glider-towing tug.

On page 41, deep within a usually overlooked aircraft of RAF Bomber Command, a wireless operator of a Handley Page Halifax tunes his radio somewhere en route to the target. Sitting directly below the pilot, this was a relatively cramped position but generally for the crew it was more spacious than that available in Bomber Command's more famous Lancaster.

Wearing flying gear typical of a late-war bomber aircrew, our pilot inspects his de Havilland Mosquito.

Our Handley Page Halifax flight engineer prepares to board.

We can tell this mission is later into World War Two given his second pattern C-Type leather flying helmet. C-Type helmets began to replace the B-type from 1941. The second pattern had internal wiring with attachments for a variety of oxygen masks. Our subject wears the G-type mask, which had oxygen and microphone attachments. His goggles were introduced in 1941 with an attachment for a coloured lens that could be dropped down in bright sun, although given the fact that Bomber Command operated primarily at night, these were often discarded.

The leather gauntlets are the 41 pattern and obscure at least two other pairs underneath. Usually, a silk pair and a chamois pair would be worn and occasionally an electrically heated pair. These go over his Sidcot flying suit, which came with a padded liner.

Over his flying suit he wears a yellow 'Mae West', an affectionate term for the life preserver. The yellow fabric was introduced from 1941 as standard based on experience during the Battle of Britain to aid with identification in the sea. It contained various survival aids including a whistle, heliograph, dye marker, a water-activated lamp, attachments for a dinghy and an inflatable stole as well as buoyant kaypok pads.

He would normally be wearing an observer-type parachute harness over this but not his actual parachute. There were various storage points for the parachute packs onboard bombers during World War Two. This meant that if the crew needed to bail out, they first had to retrieve it, clip it on and then make their way to an exit, not easy when you're in heavy kit, in the dark, at 20,000ft and potentially on fire.

Showing the equipment in full when entering an aircraft (page 41 bottom), the wireless operator peers out of the windows. In normal circumstances, he'd have parachute harness and a portable oxygen bottle to move about at high altitude, if necessary.

Above: Our Handley Page Halifax wireless operator is busy at the controls deep into a late-night mission.

Right: A full view of our Handley Page Halifax wireless operator's kit.

The RAF's four-engine bombers typically housed seven crew members during a typical operation. The pilot sat in a chair with armoured plating behind his head, just behind the nose of the aircraft. There was no co-pilot; since 1942, the flight engineer had replaced this role to conserve costs. The excessive losses of crew on dangerous bombing missions had made it impossible to supply two trained pilots for every aircraft. The flight engineer occupied a fold-out seat to the right of the pilot, from where he would monitor instruments and assist with throttle controls.

The rest of the crew was made up of two gunners, a bomb-aimer, navigator, and a wireless operator. The bomb-aimer was responsible for manning the front guns until he would adopt the prone position to peer through the sight on immediate approach to the target. There would also be a mid-gunner on the lookout for enemy aircraft, with his unique view in the upper turret. The navigator occupied a tight space where he would pour over maps and compasses with limited assistance from temperamental electronic aids. The wireless operator would monitor in-coming communications and relay messages to base, if required. Finally, the rear-gunner sat at the tail end of the aircraft in a cold space that was too tight to even wear a parachute.

Our Handley Page Halifax pilot inspects his seat, where he will be sitting for the next five hours on a long mission, going deep into enemy territory.

Above left: Our rear gunner is ready in position; his flying suit will not prevent the cold from creeping in.

Above right: Our bomb-aimer in the prone position at the front of the aircraft.

The crews of RAF Bomber Command suffered one of the highest casualty rates of World War Two. Of the 125,000 aircrew that served, just over 55,000 were killed, a death rate of over 44 per cent. Additionally, around 8,000 men were wounded in action, while almost 10,000 were captured and became prisoners of war. Even with a bit of luck, the flights were not easy: the kit was heavy and cumbersome and did barely enough to keep the crew warm. Each team of aircrew was expected to undertake 30 operations to complete their tour, and every mission was fraught with danger and discomfort. The role of the bomber aircrews is often overlooked in favour of the more glamourous fighter pilots, but without their sacrifice, the outcome of the war would have been very different.

By the middle of August 1944, after almost three months of battle following the D-Day invasion, the Allies had liberated Paris and now prepared to advance and put an end to the war. The Allies planned to enter Germany to meet Soviet troops advancing from the East. Although the fighting would continue at great cost, the outcome of the war now seemed inevitable. Bomber Command continued its aerial bombardment of Germany at pace. Meanwhile, the fighters would continue to sweep the skies.

After a difficult operation, our navigator reflects on more lost friends.

A fighter pilot from late World War Two operating from Northern France studies a map (see page 45). With similar flying equipment to the members of Bomber Command, he wears the two-piece aircrew suit made from Serge fabric displaying the rank of sergeant. For personal protection, he carries either a Webley or Enfield .38 calibre six-round revolver. Pilots of the 2nd Tactical Airforce operating from France after the Normandy Landings on 6 June 1944 were similarly attired but had a mixture of kit, including khaki serge battledress, similar to that of the army. Some mixed the clothes with khaki trousers and blue serge jacket. There were various types of boots as well, such as the 1943 pattern 'escape' boots that allowed the tops to be removed leaving a pair of black shoes.

On 8 May 1945, Germany surrendered and World War Two in Europe came to an end. Joyous crowds gathered all over Britain on a day that Churchill christened Victory in Europe (VE) Day. However, the fighting for many continued in the Far East until the eventual surrender of Japan on 2 September 1945. The war was truly devastating, and the damage and loss of life was felt long after the fighting ended. Although aerial warfare had developed considerably in World War One, this was the first conflict in which aircrews played a major role, on par with the armies and navies.

RAF Pilots' Kit During World War Two; Part 2 (1943–45)

Right and below: **The kit of a late World War Two pilot operating out of Northern France.**

Chapter 5

Post-World War Two Pilots' Kit (1945–52)

During World War Two, British engineer Frank Whittle and his team were pursuing his idea of a jet-propulsion engine. He had first pitched the idea to the Air Ministry in 1929, but it was reluctant to take up the fantastical idea. It was not until the war was well underway the idea was taken seriously. Eventually, after years of hard work, the RAF was able to introduce its first jet-powered aircraft into service – the Gloster Meteor. This development unlocked further potential in the capabilities of flight, offering more speed and altitude and almost unlimited possibilities. Of course, this new leap in technology provided an opportunity for new kit innovations to withstand these new challenges.

The Meteor first flew in 1943 and commenced operations on 27 July 1944. Thousands of Meteors were built to fly with the RAF, and many air forces across the world used them for several decades. During the 1950s, the Meteor became increasingly obsolete and was replaced by newer jets such as the Hawker Hunter and Gloster Javelin. Most were phased out of frontline service across the world by the mid-1960s, but some remained as target tugs until the 1980s.

The Gloster Meteor was the first jet-powered aircraft to enter RAF service

Our pilot climbs into his Gloster Meteor – the RAF's first jet-powered fighter.

Two meteor pilots from the late 1940s discuss their training route. Note the seat-type parachute worn by the pilot on the right.

This picture (below) shows a Gloster Meteor pilot from the immediate post-war period. The Meteor was introduced at the very end of World War Two, seeing limited service in Europe in the final months of the conflict. After the war, Britain led the world with jet technology and many countries placed orders for the Meteor. The aircraft formed the backbone of the RAF's fighter strength into the early 1950s when technological advances began to overtake the early jets. These fighters were stationed at home and in the newly formed RAF Germany in the late 1940s and began to spread out across the world as newer aircraft were procured for the RAF.

On his head, the pilot in the image on page 47 wears the C-type flying helmet, which is the second pattern with internal wiring. He wears the RAF Mk VIII goggles, which would see service with some aircrew into the 1950s. The oxygen mask is the H-type, which, by this stage, was standard for all aircrew. This had been introduced in February 1944 as a high-altitude mask for use in Mosquitos and photo reconnaissance Spitfires.

The H-type was probably the longest-lived oxygen mask used by the RAF. It was still being used for training and on the Shackleton aircraft with the RAF until the mid-1980s. It was like the preceding G-mask but with a smaller microphone. Two press-studs on its left-hand side secured it to the flying helmet, with a loop on the other securing it to a hook on the right-hand side of the flying helmet. H-Types were used with the C, F and G-type flying helmets post war.

It was common for aircrew to wear a shirt and tie in the period immediately after World War Two, as the rigours of combat were no longer present and pilots had time to ensure they always looked their best. Over his uniform, this pilot wears a new lightweight flying suit introduced initially for use over the jungle in 1945, known as the 'Beadon'. This started to become standard for aircrew when pressurisation and heated cockpits meant large padded flying suits became unnecessary. Made from a lightweight, light blue coloured cotton, the Beadon had breast

Our pilot stands next to the Gloster Meteor at the Yorkshire Air Museum.

The shirt, tie and flying suit are evident in this closer shot of our pilot by the Gloster Meteor.

pockets as well as leg pockets at various intervals to stash things such as maps and survival equipment.

His yellow life preserver is the 1941 pattern version from World War Two. The parachute harness is the standard seat-type produced by Irvin. In these early days of jets, there were no ejection seats and as such, a pilot would have to attempt to bail out as best he could but at much higher speeds than in World War Two. Finally, our pilot has leather flying gloves (this style having been introduced in 1941) to keep him warm, give him some protection should the aircraft catch fire and to stop sweat making controls difficult to use.

In cold weather, pilots still retained their 'bomber jackets' (see image on the right) in the early years after World War Two. During the Berlin Airlift of 1948–49 crews can be seen wearing Beadons with the Irvin bomber jacket over the top. Most were in large, troop/freight-carrying aircraft that were not pressurised or heated. Seeing the value of such suits, the RAF developed these further as pilot feedback indicated the value of these designs for their needs. Because of the better conditions, some pilots elected to wear shoes rather than flying boots.

Whilst the RAF's fighter pilots got to grips with their new jet fighters, the bomber and transport crews concentrated on humanitarian operations during this period. In 1948, the Soviets created a blockade that prevented access via road and rail to the Western-controlled areas of Berlin. The RAF formed the backbone of the aerial missions to keep the civilians in the area supplied with food and essentials. The Berlin Airlift, as it came to be known, went on for nearly a year with round-the-clock missions taking place to deliver vital supplies to the blockaded Berliners. For crews taking off on the continent or near to the Eastern Sector borders, life preservers

Now ready for flight, our pilot prepares to taxi out on to the runway.

During colder conditions, flight crews would wear their bomber jackets – here they stand in front of a Gloster Meteor T7, which was based at Coventry Airport before moving to the United States in 2018.

were unnecessary, and in the summer months, cold weather gear at relatively low altitudes was discarded.

Standing in a Dakota, in the image below, a pilot assesses the situation before the next flight. Wearing the standard headgear for a temperate climate in this period, the C-type with an H-Type mask and Mk VIII goggles. Note the lack of an oxygen tube on the mask, which was common during some operations. Although not seen, it's likely that he wears the 1941 pattern flying boots.

His jacket is a recent addition to the RAF uniform. Introduced in 1947, the 'Aircrew Suits New Pattern' jacket started to be issued gradually to personnel, although it was common to see older variants in use. This would be replaced by the 1951 pattern jacket, which was similar in appearance but with a slightly different collar. The 1947 pattern was tailored with an open collar but could be closed, if needed, whereas the 1951 design did not allow for this. On his jacket is a short-lived badge from the new method of rank insignia introduced in 1946, which was later made obsolete in 1950. These badges were issued to aircrew ranks only. Three six-pointed stars in a wreath and surmounted by a crown denoted the rank of Aircrew 1, which was the equivalent to a flight sergeant.

In the immediate period following World War Two, changes in pilots' kit were slow to progress. Although the arrival of jet aircraft provided new challenges, many pilots clung on to their favoured kit

Our pilot is on board the Douglas Dakota, ready to deliver supplies to Berlin in 1948.

Our pilot arrives in Berlin, receiving a warmer welcome than he would have done three years earlier.

that had seen them through the hostile actions. They were reluctant to change kit that had got them through difficult times. However, as jet technology progressed, the performance of aircraft vastly improved, putting pilots and aircrew under considerable strain with high g loads. New technology was clearly needed to protect the human body under these circumstances.

Chapter 6
RAF Second Generation Jet Pilot Kit (1952–59)

The 1950s was an exciting decade for the RAF; it saw the end of service for many of its iconic propellor-driven World War Two aircraft such as the Lancaster, Mosquito and Spitfire. All of these were replaced by new jet-powered aircraft including the Supermarine Swift, English Electric Canberra and the Hawker Hunter. Meanwhile, the Cold War began, leaving the RAF in a constant state of alert of a Soviet attack. Fortunately, the Cold War did not turn hot.

The English Electric Canberra was the RAF's first jet-powered bomber to enter military service. It was first conceived in the mid-1940s in response to the Air Ministry's request for a replacement for the de Havilland Mosquito. Amongst its many qualities was its capability to operate at very high altitude at high speeds in comparison to other medium bomber aircraft at the time. The Canberra broke many records including the first jet-powered non-stop transatlantic flight and a series of high-altitude records, peaking at over 70,000ft in 1957.

At the beginning of the jet age, little distinction was made between the kit of a fighter or bomber pilot, despite the differences in the types of operation undertaken. In the images on page 54 we see that the Canberra pilot's kit is very close to that worn by pilots of the Swift, but to aid high-altitude operations he is wearing a J-type oxygen mask. The Canberra would regularly operate at heights above 40,000ft, where pressure breathing was necessary due to the lower air pressure. To meet the contradictory requirements of low breathing resistance, a rotating knob was incorporated in the valve housing, which would adjust the spring tension when required. This newly designed mask became the J-Type, although issues were still experienced with the mask sealing around the face.

Our pilot is now ready for the age of the swept-wing jet, complete with hard-shell Mk 1 flying helmet, Mk VIII goggles and anti-g trousers (also known as 'speed jeans').

Our pilot prepares his J-type oxygen mask ready for a high-altitude sortie in his English Electric Canberra.

RAF Second Generation Jet Pilot Kit (1952–59)

The Supermarine Swift featured many of the new jet-age innovations on the airframe itself and for its pilots. It was one of the RAF's first swept-wing fighters, which unlocked the potential for considerably more speed than the straight-winged first generation of jets, which included the Meteor and Vampire. In 1953, the Swift achieved a world absolute speed record of 737.7mph. It entered RAF service as an interceptor in 1954. Several accidents incurred by the type led to the Swift being grounded for a time, and, as such, it experienced a relatively brief service life, but its new performance capabilities made it a significant type in the story of RAF kit. Flying at over 700mph puts significant pressure on the human body, particularly during tight turns. Although a photo reconnaissance variant of the Swift resolved some of the teething problems, it came too late for it to regain favour. In total, 197 were built before they were retired in 1967.

This pilot (right) wears the most modern equipment for the mid-1950s. Until the early 1950s, there was no head protection available to pilots. The leather C-Type flying helmets of World War Two vintage were more of a way to hold the headphones onto the head than giving any meaningful protection. With the speeds of aircraft increasing, the hard-shell helmets, known affectionately by pilots as 'bone domes', sought to do two things, firstly to provide protection in the event of an accident and secondly to provide a small amount of ballistic protection if a pilot was to come under fire.

The helmet is the Mk 1A. Whilst the goggle and visor arrangement were satisfactory enough, a further modification was made to the MK 1 shell to make eye protection easier. A track was added along the centre from front to back, and on to this a visor was added. It could be raised and lowered easily by pushing down on the white plastic fitting on the tack to lower it and by pulling backwards to raise it. The Mk 1A would see service all through the 1960s, and in some cases into the '70s, with later examples being finished in green. There are some pictures from the 1970s of Vulcan rear crew members using these alongside G-type flying helmets to give them more space, no doubt, in the confined space at the back.

Under the bone dome, this pilot wears a G-type inner helmet. The introduction of the G-type appears to coincide with the introduction of the Swift. New oxygen masks had been in development to replace the high-altitude J mask. The development of the M-type oxygen mask with its three-point fitting on its right-hand side necessitated extra studs being added on both sides of the face.

With aircraft reaching ever greater altitudes and speeds in the 1950s, there was a real danger that, should the aircraft decompress,

Our pilot demonstrates all the latest 1950s innovations in pilots' gear, including the new hard-shell Mk 1A helmet and M-type oxygen mask.

or if the pilot/crew needed to eject at high altitude, the body would not cope with the conditions, leading to the blood boiling. To prevent this, a pressure waistcoat was introduced and that led to the development of the jerkin. Working in a similar way to the anti-g trousers, the initial waistcoat design would lace up at the back and had a mounting point on the right breast for a regulator to connect on to the J- and M-type oxygen masks. The small square holes found on the right-hand side of the life preservers allowed the connector to protrude though it allowing connection to the oxygen tube.

With the increase in speed and manoeuvrability came an increase in g-force. In tight turns, blood tended to rush to the legs and out of the head and torso, which could cause the pilot to black out. Trousers were introduced that would fill with air, squeezing the legs and waist to prevent this. They have a similar sensation on the body as a blood pressure device does upon the arm. In the image on page 55, they are worn over the flying suit, which was common at the time. Laces that could be tightened ran down each side of the trousers. They were fastened with a zip on both legs and straps at the waist.

The anti-g-trousers were designed to inflate pneumatically during flight. They have a series of five bladders that press on five different areas of the body (the calves, thighs and abdomen). When inflated, they tighten the material around the sides and back of the leg, which prevents pooling of the blood in the feet and legs and also maintains blood pressure to the heart and brain. The trousers were cut-out around the knees and groin to allow mobility.

With the RAF introducing ejection seats, it was found that pilots' legs would flail about whilst the torso would be held rigid in the seat. Early ejection seats shot the pilot backwards at an angle. If the aircraft was in level flight, this would almost be at 45 degrees. As newer marks became available that could allow the pilot to eject on the ground and send him vertically, there was a danger that, on exit, his legs could hit the interior and break. To overcome this, leg garters or restraints began to be issued. These could be adjusted with the aid of a buckle and Velcro and would clip around the leg. A loop, or loops, on them allowed for the passage of a retention strap that on ejection would tighten and draw in the legs tightly until safely away from the aircraft. These became standard for air crew using ejection seats from the 1950s.

The Hawker Hunter was designed around the new Rolls-Royce Avon turbojet engine and swept-wing concept. It was

Our pilot wears the new pressure waistcoat.

the first successful jet aircraft developed by the famous Hawker Siddeley Aircraft and would go on to be one of its most well-respected aircraft. Various companies were grappling with new designs, such as Supermarine with the Swift, and, although quick, it was dangerous, but Hawker seemed to be on a winner, with the Hunter, selling it to different air forces across the world. First flying in 1951, it eventually entered RAF service in 1954. It became the primary interceptor of the RAF until the introduction of the Lightning in the 1960s, when its role changed to reconnaissance and that of a fighter-bomber. It was withdrawn as a front-line aircraft in the RAF in 1967 but continued to be used as a trainer.

The helmet worn by the pilot in the image below is a Mk 1A with attached visor being operated by a central track running from front to back on the helmet. The inner helmet is the F-type, with the oxygen mask based on the American A-13 but with a British external microphone, making this an A-13A1. His suit is tucked into a pair of 1952 pattern flying boots. These were a variant of the 1943 escape boots. In this instance, with the aid of a knife, the pilot could remove the tops and be left with a pair of shoes. This style of boot would continue into the 1960s. The life preserver is a Mk2, with equipment like that of the 1941 pattern.

Our pilot stands in front of the RAF Museum's Hawker Hunter gate guardian at RAF Museum Midlands in Cosford.

Our later Hawker Hunter pilot with Mk 2 flying helmet and Mk 9 flying suit.

A rather proud-looking pilot of a Vickers Valiant poses for a publicity shot sometime in the late 1950s.

The Hawker Hunter was a long-lived and incredibly successful aircraft, and as the Hunter was modified, so too was the pilot's kit. In the image on page 58, the pilot is wearing a Mk 2 flying helmet with Mk 9 flying suit. He is also wearing an A-13A1 oxygen mask. The attachment on the base of the hose originates from America, where it was used on the North American F-86 Sabre jet that was adopted by the RAF while it awaited the next generation of British jets. When they entered service, the Hawker Hunter and Percival Jet Provost also used this set up.

In 1946, in the firm belief that possession and the ability to deploy a nuclear weapon was the only way to remain a major player in the world stage, the British military issued a specification for a high-performance, long-range bomber capable of carrying a nuclear weapon. The Air Ministry recognised the complexity of developing a new bomber to meet the specification, and although it favoured the submissions by Avro and Handley Page, it knew that designs by those manufacturers would take longer to come to fruition. The ministry therefore selected the more conventional swept-wing Vickers Type 600 project as a faster, stop-gap solution, even though it failed to meet all requirements in the brief. The Vickers 600 became known as the Valiant and was the first to

Our early V-Force pilot stands in front of the only remaining Vickers Valiant, which appears at the RAF Museum in Cosford in anti-flash white. This was the first British aircraft to drop an atomic bomb.

enter service, arriving at squadrons from 1955. However, just ten years later, when tactics switched from high altitude to low-altitude bombing runs, the Valiant began to show dangerous signs of fatigue on the airframe and was subsequently withdrawn.

In the image on page 59, a Valiant crew member stands near his aircraft in full kit. Of note here is his parachute harness with the release handle visible on his left shoulder. Rear crew members in all the V-Force aircraft had parachutes rather than ejection seats. He wears a Mk 2 flying suit and Mk 3 life preserver. His helmet is a Mk 1. The inner is a G-type with an A-13A2 oxygen mask with skeleton harness that allows it to be dropped down from the face but remain attached on both sides preventing difficulty in reattaching it to the side as in earlier models.

Although the RAF aircraft of the 1950s like the Hawker Hunter and English Electric Canberra were superb aircraft designs and, in many ways, ahead of their time, they were all transonic. The latest aircraft designs from all over the world were now capable of exceeding the speed of sound in level flight, and if the RAF was to keep up, it would need new, faster aircraft. This, in turn, would put further demands on the pilot and the kit would need to evolve alongside it.

Our Hawker Hunter pilot looks to the skies, considering his next flight.

Chapter 7

RAF Third Generation Jet Pilot Kit (1960–69)

By the end of the 1950s, the threat of a nuclear strike from the USSR was ever-growing, and the development of jet-powered aircraft all over the world was continuing at a pace. If the RAF was to be able to maintain its protection of the British Isles, it would need ever-faster aircraft that could fly above and beyond the speed of sound to intercept Soviet bombers before they could deliver their payload.

Entering squadron service in December 1959, the English Electric Lightning was the RAF's most technologically advanced fighter to date. The early aircraft were equipped with both ADEN Cannon guns and air-to-air de Havilland Firestreak missiles. Lightnings could cruise comfortably at over twice the speed of sound. It was the last all-British interceptor capable of that speed to enter RAF service.

In the image on the left, the pilot is wearing the Mk 2 flying suit introduced in the mid-1950s, though it is obscured by a pressure jerkin. It differed from the Mk 1 suit by having zipped slash pockets on the chest, as opposed to patch pockets with buttoned flaps. Above the left-hand side pocket is a small loop intended to attach a clip from the base of the oxygen mask to take the weight off, prolonging its serviceability if a life preserver was not required. On the right knee was a space for a white board covered in clear plastic. This allowed the pilot to write notes with a chinagraph pencil during briefings, alter them and then after a sortie, erase them.

Over the flight suit is a pressure jerkin. A development of the pressure waistcoat as worn by the Swift pilot; this style was gradually introduced in the late 1950s. There is an internal stole to allow it to expand with air. In order to don the garment, the pilot had to step into the right leg and then lift it up, putting both arms

Our English Electric Lightning pilot poses next to the Yorkshire Air Museum's F6 variant.

Our Lightning pilot prepares to climb into the cockpit wearing full anti-g protection with his Mk 2 suit and pressure jerkin.

through before zipping it from the neck to around the left leg. It contained the same items as a standard life preserver. The orange/yellow cover around his neck is his built-in life vest.

On the right-hand side of the pilot there is a hose. This would be attached to his Personal Equipment Connector (PEC). Connecting to the ejection seat, the PEC had connectors for oxygen, communications, an air-ventilated suit and anti-g trousers. This was a quick way to plug all of the vital components into the aircraft at once. Because he wears a pressure jerkin, there is a connector part way down that screws into the jerkin itself. The jerkin was regulated by the pilot's own breathing as different pilots would react in different ways to the conditions. The PEC would attach on different sides of the pilot depending on the aircraft he was flying and/or which mark of ejection seat was in the aircraft. To allow the hose from the g-trousers to attach on to the PEC there is a small rectangular aperture on the pressure jerkin near the thigh to allow it to come through the flying suit and the jerkin. This air-ventilated suit would be worn underneath the flying suit and the g-trousers.

The pilot's headgear is the Mk 2 flying helmet, introduced in the early 1960s. The main problem with the previous designs – Mk 1 and Mk 1A – was that the pilot had two separate components on his head. The inner F and G types were not connected, and as such the hard shell could potentially slip about. This was addressed for the fast jets with the Mk 2, which had built-in headphones and an easier visor system. The track on the MK 1A could occasionally stick, which could be quite dangerous. A thin yellow bar ran across the front of the helmet, which allowed the visor to drop far quicker and easier and meant there was no danger of potentially pulling the front down over the eyes! The visor was also a different shape. The previous ones were cut straight across the face, whereas the Mk 2 had a goggle shape to them. This allowed it to sit better over the bridge of the nose and the oxygen mask. These helmets continued in service until well into the 1970s, being produced in green rather than white.

Our Lightning pilot, wearing the Mk 2 helmet.

The oxygen mask worn by the pilot in the image on page 64 is the P-type, which has two small chains with a loop at each end to attach to the hooks on the inner helmet. The P-type was issued from around 1959/60 as a replacement for the high-altitude, fast jet M-type. Undergoing minor modifications (mainly with the microphone and electrics), it was still being issued in the 1980s. To secure it over the face, the air crew member would place the mask over his nose and mouth and then pull down the hinged mechanism on the front tightening the chains. At its base, to provide a stronger seal, was another small, hinged plate which would seal the mask tightly over the pilot's face. Note the leg restraints for the ejector seat, white leather gloves and the 1952 pattern flying boots.

By the end of the 1960s, new equipment began to be issued to Lightning crews, with the pressure jerkins being gradually phased out, flying suits upgraded, and newer boots and more hard-wearing life preservers becoming standard.

In the photograph below, this pilot wears the Mk 9 flying suit made from lighter weight material. His boots are the 1965 pattern. Whilst the helmet, oxygen mask, gloves and PEC remain the same, his life preserver (a Mk 9) is produced entirely of nylon for the first time, providing a longer service life as it is less likely to get ripped and torn when compared to the previous cotton ones. Although the blue colouring would appear to be difficult to pick out in water, on pulling the handle to inflate the stole, it would open into a bright orange colour to help with locating a downed pilot.

Our Lightning pilot wears the newer, more hard-wearing life preserver.

Lightnings were finally stood down in the RAF in 1988 after nearly 29 years' service. For an interceptor, and, considering the advance in technology, this was a remarkable feat. The strategic defence strategy for the United Kingdom had shifted, and there was no longer the need for a fast take-off, high speed interceptor, instead an aircraft capable of more efficient patrols of British airspace

Following his flight, our Lightning pilot reflects on his days in the best fighter to serve with the RAF to date.

were deemed more important. Additionally, the likelihood of a surprise nuclear attack had all but diminished and with it the need for an aircraft like the English Electric Lightning.

In 1969, the McDonnell Douglas F-4 Phantom entered RAF service. This was a US-designed and built aircraft, although the UK version incorporated a significant amount of British technology. The Phantom had several advantages over the Lightning as it could carry more fuel, and had consequently better range and endurance. The Phantom served between 1969 and 1992 and filled several roles, including air defence, close-air support, low-level strike and tactical reconnaissance. The Phantom brought change for RAF crew and, with it, upgraded kit and a different approach to pilot safety.

In these early stages of Phantom introduction, there was a mixture of headgear in use including the Mk 2, 2A and 3B helmets. The P-type oxygen mask was now standard for most aircrew of fast jets. On his chest is a man-mounted oxygen regulator, which reduces the fitting of the oxygen hose for the PEC connector. This PEC had a much narrower base or shoe than previous designs. The PEC runs down the left-hand side of the pilot. The thicker, lighter coloured tube connects to a pair of Mk 6 internal anti-g trousers.

Introduced in the late 1960s, he wears a turtleneck long sleeve T-shirt in NATO green under a Mk 11 flying suit. Mk 11 and 12 flying suits seem to have been issued to coincide with the Phantom trials of 1967. The Mk 12 was similar to the Mk 11 in cut but was issued specifically to the Royal Navy, which also operated Phantoms. This suit falls over the top of his 1965 pattern flying boots.

Over the flying suit is either a Mk 10 or 11 life preserver. The harness attached within altered the stock code numbers for the garment but remained the same mark of lifesaving jacket. The difference in numbering stems from the types of survival aids carried within it. Based on designs from the United

The RAF Museum's McDonnell Douglas F-4 Phantom, on display at Hendon, is shown in late 1980s livery.

Before heading out to his waiting Phantom, a pilot of 43 Squadron 'The Fighting Cocks', signs for his aircraft at RAF Leuchars in late 1969.

States Air Force (USAF), which had been using the Phantom since the early 1960s, the life preserver incorporated a harness that would fit directly into the parachute within the ejection seat. Entering service as a fast interceptor in the days of Quick Reaction Alert (QRA), every second saved on the ground was vital in meeting the enemy somewhere over the North Sea. Climbing into his seat, the crew of a Phantom would be strapped in by a member of the groundcrew, ready to meet the threat.

Chapter 8
RAF Pilots' Kit During the 1970s

The 1970s was a relativity peaceful time for the RAF. Although the threat of the Cold War remained, the nuclear deterrent role was handed over to the Royal Navy's Polaris submarines. The RAF were far from idle during this period, however. For example, Operation *Khana Cascade* was the biggest airlift to take place since Berlin, when RAF Hercules crews dropped over 2,000 tons of grain, maize and rice to famine-hit areas of Nepal in 1973. At that time, the government, however, was re-evaluating British military requirements and as such spending cuts and changes were made. The RAF would be taking on new roles as the country's defence strategies were rewritten. With this, there would be a transition from aircraft like the Lighting and V-bombers, which had been designed to counter a possible Soviet threat, towards newer aircraft capable of supporting missions closer to home came next.

Returning from a successful training flight, in the image below, the five-man crew of a Vulcan make their way to a crew bus sometime in the 1970s. The early 1970s was a period of massive change for

The crew of an Avro Vulcan following a night-time training sortie in the early 1970s.

Our five-man crew of an Avro Vulcan return to the crew bus following a successful flight in the mid-1970s.

the RAF and alongside was the transition to all-green kit. The RAF of the 1970s was relatively small compared to other air forces.

From right to left, there is a member of the rear crew then a pilot, a second pilot and two further members of the rear crew although their specifics roles are hard to determine as their life preservers obscure their insignia. The give-away sign of pilots is the leg restraints and PECs with a shoe to fit in their ejection seats. Rear crew had to make do with a parachute harness and attempt to jump if the need to bail out arose.

The flying suits (again from right to left) are a Mk 11, two Mk 9s, another Mk 11 and a further Mk 9, all in green. Flying helmets from right to left are two green Mk 1As with green G-type inners and P-type masks. The helmet being carried by the third from the right is a green Mk 2, next is a white Mk 1A with G-type inner and the last member has a white Mk 3C. Life preservers are Mk 17s, introduced in the 1970s. All wear the long sleeve turtleneck T-shirts with 1965 pattern boots. The gloves are all-white kid leather.

In the image on page 70, two crew members have a tea break next to a practice bomb and assorted kit. This is a recreation of a typical posed image from the time when aircrew would wear caps or sit on dummy bombs for the cameras. Caps would not be permitted on live airfields due to presenting

Two Vulcan crew members have a tea break next to a practice bomb and assorted kit.

a risk of foreign object debris, known as FOD. From left to right, there is a 'Nav' bag with maps and navigation equipment, a yellow survival pack, a green helmet bag in front of a larger temperate survival pack for multiple crew members, a beige helmet bag, a green Mk 3C helmet and another Nav bag. Of note here are the Mk 3 Cold Weather Jackets, one from the 1960s in blue/grey and a later example in green. The seated crew member is also wearing a blue collared shirt and cravat, still a common sight in the early 1970s.

In 1972, the RAF's first Airborne Early-Warning Squadron (No 8 Squadron at Kinloss) was formed, consisting of the Avro Shackleton AEW Mk 2. The Shackleton was essentially a development of the Avro Lancaster but with Griffon engines and the latest radar technology. The squadron was formed to patrol around the British Isles on constant look-out for threats. The Shackleton was developed in the late 1940s and entered RAF service in 1951. It had a very long career but was eventually retired in 1991.

Shackleton flights over the North Sea and North Atlantic could be several hours and could get extremely cold. On page 72, the pilot's equipment consists of a Mk 9 flying suit, which was manufactured in both blue and green and falls over the top of a pair of 1965 pattern flying boots. As was still common for this period, he wears his standard light blue RAF shirt under the suit. He is also wearing a Mk 4A life preserver.

Avro Shackleton MR2 WR963, seen here at Coventry Airport during an evening engine run.

    He wears his observer parachute harness dating from the interwar period in pattern but with several updates, including an improved black quick release buckle and light brown webbing straps. He carries the parachute for the harness in his right hand. This has two metal loops on the rear that clip on to the front of the harness before bailing out of the aircraft. When the handle is pulled, the parachute canopy opens and begins to fill with air, pulling the C clips of the harness out of their cradle and sending them above the head. The pack on his rear is a personal survival pack. This clips on to two connectors on the life preserver and carries basic aids should he need them. All aircrew went on survival courses that trained them to use the equipment packs as well as how to use objects from the immedieate surroundings to stay alive until rescue came.

    In his left hand, he carries a Nav bag with various maps, charts and individual manuals appertaining to his specific role onboard. On the outside of this is his flying helmet. Not usually worn in the aircraft, the hard-shell Mk 1A had a storage place above the seat of each crew member along the main bank of instruments. The inner G-type, in this instance a green one, would be worn on its own providing the headphones to hear the rest of the crew. His oxygen mask would be the H-type as used by the Meteor pilot but with an updated microphone. Clutched in his hand are a pair of white flying gloves.

Above left: A member of the RAF airborne early warning team heads out to join the rest of the crew of a Mk 2 Shackleton in the early 1970s.

Above right: Our Shackleton crew member on his way to join the rest of the crew. Note the personal survival pack

Left: Our Shackleton crew member walks past the control tower, ready for the sortie.

Our Shackleton crew member is now ready to board his aircraft.

As the 1970s were ending, the British military was under further review and all the armed forces were facing cuts. The RAF was undergoing major changes, with many of its aircraft approaching the end of their service lives. The new strategy was in line with that of NATO, and the main goal was to protect British mainline airspace and to support NATO operations. No one foresaw a war on British territory on the other side of the world.

Chapter 9
RAF Pilots' Kit During the 1980s and the Falklands War

In 1982, an ongoing dispute between the Argentine and British governments over the ownership of a group of Islands in the South Atlantic reached boiling point when a group claiming to be Argentine scrap metal merchants raised the Argentine flag on South Georgia. This act is now considered the first offensive action of the Falklands War. The Royal Navy quickly despatched its nearest asset, the ice patrol vessel HMS *Endurance* in response. Foreseeing a large-scale response from British forces, the Argentine government quickly ordered *Operation Rosario,* and on 2 April 1982 undertook an amphibious invasion of the Falkland Islands, South Georgia and the South Sandwich Islands. The British task force sent to retake the islands faced a logistical nightmare, as there were more than 8,000 miles between the Falklands and the British mainland.

Fortunately, a remote volcanic Island and British territory called Ascension Island was located approximately halfway between Britain and the Falklands. During the 1920s, a single runway, known as Wideawake Airfield, was installed there to assist transatlantic military and civilian logistics. At 10,000ft, the runway was just about long enough for the take-off and landing of the largest aircraft in the RAF at the time.

The crew of a Lockheed C130 Hercules discuss the flight plan.

Apart from aircraft designed as long-range airliners, such as the Vickers VC10, most of the RAF, Army Air Corps and Federal Aviation Authority (FAA) aircraft were not capable of reaching the South Atlantic without either a lift on an aircraft carrier or support from air-to-air refuelling aircraft. While other aircraft including the Vickers VC10s were converted into tanking aircraft, most of the air-to-air refuelling work was carried out by the Handley Page Victor. The Lockheed Hercules aircraft were given additional fuel tanks and became the first propeller-driven aircraft in service with air-to-air refuelling probes as standard. These modifications allowed the transport to deliver essential supplies and equipment to the South Atlantic.

The Handley Page Victor was one of the three V-bombers developed during the 1950s. Like the Avro Vulcan, it was nearing the end of its operational career but had found a new lease of life as a tanker. Following its work in 1982, the Victor would continue in service for another ten years after the Falklands campaign and would even see action in the First Gulf War.

Right: Our VC10 co-pilot undertakes a radio check prior to departure.

Below: Leaning casually, a pilot of a Victor tanker appears to be waiting for the rest of his crew.

Certain elements of his equipment are the same as those in previous pictures, such as the life preserver, oxygen mask, PEC, leg restraints and boots. The flying suit is a Mk 14 made from Nomex, a flame-resistant material introduced in the early 1970s. His gloves are the green version made of kid leather, and he wears a green Mk 3C helmet. The green tab hanging from the life preserver is to clip into his survival pack.

The Avro Vulcan was one of Britain's famous V-bombers designed in the 1950s to deliver Britain's nuclear weapons. It was operational in the RAF from 1956, initially as a high-altitude bomber, but as the demands of the Cold War shifted, it was switched to a low-level bomber. At the time of the Falkland's War, the ageing Vulcans were heading for retirement, having never been used in conflict. Incredibly, when Argentina invaded the Falkland Islands, some of the remaining air frames were quickly deployed to Ascension Island to undertake the *Black Buck* bombing raids. At the time, these missions were the longest bombing runs in history, the success of which ensured the reputation of the Vulcan, which today remains one of the most revered aircraft ever developed in Britain.

In the image below, the pilot on the ladder is wearing a privately purchased Cold Weather Jacket, produced by Alpha but closely modelled on the RAF issue. Green had taken over by this time for official issue, but Alpha still produced them in blue. The middle crew member is a 'back seater' wearing a Multi-Service Connector for oxygen and communications rather than the PEC that connected to the ejection seat. He also wears a G-type inner helmet in green with his MK 1A bone dome in his left hand. These early helmets are occasionally seen in period photos with rear crew members; its design provided more space in very cramped conditions. In the background, a ground crew member manoeuvres a practice WE177 free-fall nuclear bomb into position.

During the Falklands War, protection of the British task force was dependent on the fleet of sub-sonic V/STOL (Vertical/short take-off and landing) aircraft, the Hawker Siddeley (later British

Three members of a Vulcan from the 1980s begin their climb to the cockpit.

Aerospace) Harrier. During the Falklands campaign, the Royal Navy operated its purpose-built Sea Harrier FRS1 variant in an almost constant combat air patrol over the task force. Every available Sea Harrier was sent to the conflict, and additionally British Aerospace were encouraged to finish any aircraft on the production line as quickly as possible. More Harriers were still required and as such, the RAF hastily adapted its GR3 Harriers to operate from the decks of the Navy's carriers. These RAF aircraft were mainly operated in a ground-attack role during the war, as their radar and electronics were not optimised for operations over sea.

Harriers provided the unique capability of vertical take-off and landing if required, and as such, provided a huge tactical advantage on the battlefield. Capable of taking off from conventional runways, they also operated out of camouflaged hides in Britain and the Federal Republic of Germany during the Cold War. Groundcrew wore similar camouflaged patterns to the army when operating from these hides, and RAF pilots took precautions to blend in, such as the green kid gloves, which were used by army and RAF helicopter pilots.

The pilot (below) wears the MK 3C flying helmet introduced in the early 1970s. The Mk 3A and Mk 3B had a visor with a single track like the old Mk 1As of the Hunter and Swift pilots seen earlier but with internal headphones like the Mk2. The Mk3 series of helmets were produced in both green and white. The oxygen mask has the same mouth and nose covering as the P-type but with a different hose and connector.

The PEC for this aircraft was much thinner than previous designs such as the Phantom but worn on the right-hand side of the pilot. Also, like the Phantom pilot, he wears a man-mounted regulator, a 317, attached to a Mk 22 life preserver. This was like the one in the Phantom but used without the harness. His flying suit is the Mk 11 but this time is obscured by external anti-g trousers, which became more of a feature of pilots from the mid-1970s onwards. Over these he wears leg restraints. Various upgrades were made to the Harrier over its service life, and by the 1990s two pairs of leg restraints were worn with a wider PEC.

Immersion suits go all the way back to World War Two. This type was standard issue from the late 1960s until recently. The type of aircraft flown determined whether there was a black rubber outlet midway down on the front right-hand side or on the left or not at all. There were tight seals on the wrists and around the neck to stop water getting in. They had built-in rubber socks. The large zip

Our 1980s Harrier pilot is ready for flight.

Our Harrier pilot poses next to the GR3 Harrier on display at the Yorkshire Air Museum.

diagonally across the front allowed the aircrew member to get in. There was another zip on the back that allowed for expansion when donning the suit. The black outlet would be for the anti-g trouser connector. The one in the image on page 80 belonged to Grp Capt Bob Iveson, who joined the RAF in 1967. He flew Harriers from the mid-1970s and was deployed to the Falklands during the war in 1982 when the operations over the vast expanse of the South Atlantic required the use of the immersion suit.

Aircrew equipment for the RAF's larger aircraft such as the VC10, Hercules and Nimrod was broadly the same for each aircraft. The images on the following pages present the typical crew kit in use from the 1980s into the 1990s.

The Hawker Siddeley Nimrod was developed as a maritime patrol aircraft based on the basic design of the British de Havilland Comet airliner. The Comet was the world's first jet airliner, and after major issues around fatigue and compression were overcome, it became a successful aircraft. The de Havilland aircraft company began work on the project, but when the company was purchased by Hawker Siddeley in 1960 work on the Nimrod began to gather pace. In 1978, the company merged into British Aerospace, which continued work on the Nimrod, developing a successful aircraft for the RAF until its eventual retirement in 2011.

Leaving the aircraft after a long maritime reconnaissance flight in a Hawker Siddeley Nimrod, our pilot wears his cap. This was unusual for the flight line, as it could, of course, fly off and get sucked into the engines causing great damage. While wearing a cap was unacceptable during operations, many posed photoshoots show the pilots and aircrew with caps on. Our pilot wears a Mk 25 life preserver and a Mk 3 Cold Weather Jacket with a Mk 14A flight suit. He also carries a flight bag with maps and his headphones with a boom microphone. There are attachments for an oxygen mask, if required.

Above left: Group Captain Bob Iveson's Immersion suit on display at the RAF Museum in Hendon.

Above right: Our Nimrod pilot, after returning from a long maritime reconnaissance sortie.

The Vickers VC10 was designed by Vickers-Armstrong at Brooklands in Surrey as a medium-capacity jet airliner. It was designed to be fast and efficient and was capable of landing on shorter runways. It could also handle extreme weather conditions and as such was ideal for reaching and operating from remote locations. The unusual layout of engines at the rear of the aircraft was designed to give passengers a quieter experience compared to other more conventional aircraft with engines mounted in the wings. The first prototype flew in 1962, and by 1965 it began to enter service with the RAF. All the initial VC10s in RAF service were named after servicemen who had been awarded the Victoria Cross. The VC10s served with No. 10 Squadron which was operational in the support of Operation *Corporate* throughout the conflict.

The Lockheed Martin C-130 Hercules was developed in the US during the 1950s; its first flight was in 1954, and just two years later it began to enter service with the USAF. It is one of the most widely used transport aircraft of modern times and has seen extensive service with air arms all over the world including with the RAF.

Crouching in a doorway of Hercules, in the image at the bottom of page 81, a loadmaster wears the Mk 3A flying helmet, designed initially for helicopter crews, with attached boom mic. This is the later green style. An MK 25 life preserver is worn over the top as a MK 2 Cold Weather Jacket in Disruptive

Still wearing his beret, our pilot makes pre-flight checks. Of note here are his flying gloves. Green kid leather gloves were first issued in the 1970s and were commonly seen on Harrier pilots in the hides in Germany.

Busy at work, our crew member wears a headset made by Airmed Ltd of Harlow. There were various designs, and they first began to be issued in the 1950s initially for civilian use and later to the RAF. These were the standard design before the headsets in the previous pictures.

RAF Pilots' Kit During the 1980s and the Falklands War

A close up of the Airmed headset being used by a VC-10 crew member. On this more civilian-style flight for troop transport, the life preserver has been disregarded and just the flying suit remains.

Our Hercules loadmaster wears the Mk 3A flying helmet.

Pattern Material (DPM) like the army. The Mk 2s were normally issued to helicopter crews in the Army Air Corps but are occasionally seen on operations with the RAF in combat zones. The loadmaster wears standard white gloves with a Mk 14A flight suit and 1965 pattern boots. Around his waist is a harness (more like a reinforced waist belt) used by door crews and attached via a carabiner to the inside of the aircraft.

Sitting on the steps to the cockpit of a Hercules transport and dressed in a very similar manner to the previous picture, the crew member below is wearing the standard Mk 3 Cold Weather Jacket but with the same study door harness as before. The rest of the kit remains the same, but there is also a blue RAF kit bag and flight bag. On top, sits his Mk 3A helmet, and the visor still has its cover on. Note the grey boom mic.

After many operations throughout the 1980s in cold weather climates such as the Falklands campaign, the 1990s would see a new challenge for the RAF. Trouble was brewing in the Gulf, and any operations in the desert would create new challenges for RAF pilots and crew, which would mean more adjustments to the kit required.

Our Hercules crew member wears the Mk 3 Cold Weather Jacket.

Chapter 10
RAF Pilots' Kit During the 1990s and the Gulf War

In August 1990, Iraq invaded Kuwait, fully occupying the whole country within two days. The US spearheaded a coalition of 35 countries, including the United Kingdom, to liberate Kuwait. The First Gulf War would last just over six months; the British military codenamed its part of the mission Operation *Granby*. Within nine days of the invasion, 12 RAF F3 Tornados had arrived in the area, closely followed by squadrons of Jaguars and GR1 Tornados. Eventually, the ageing Buccaneers were also deployed to assist the Tornados by guiding them into targets using their laser pods, which were not fitted to any other aircraft at that time. Kuwait was eventually liberated on 28 February 1991.

The Panavia Tornado entered service in 1979 and was produced jointly by Italy, Germany and Britain. It was developed as a multi-role aircraft, designed to replace several aircraft currently in use with the RAF at the time. The Tornado served in strike, interception and reconnaissance

Above left: Our Parnavia Tornado pilot of the mid 1990s stands next to the Yorkshire Air Museum's GR1.

Above right: Our Parnavia Tornado pilot of the late 1980s is ready for a training flight.

roles, eventually replacing what was left of the V-Force bombers, English Electric Lightnings and McDonnell Douglas Phantoms. After sterling service for four decades, the Tornado was retired by the RAF in 2019.

Unsurprisingly for an aircraft in service for so long, the flying kit varied through the aircraft's career. The flying suit worn by early Tornado pilots was the Mk 14A or 14B. Mk 14s were introduced in the early 1970s but were phased out of use for fast-jet use during the 1990s in favour of the Mk 16 and 16B. The Mk 14 was made from Nomex rather than the cotton used in earlier designs. Nomex is a durable, flame-resistant material developed in the early 1960s by DuPont. It is produced using aramid polymers like Nylon but with a more rigid structure, making it ideal for the everyday wear and tear experienced during the modern pilot's schedule.

This style of equipment was identical to that issued in the First Gulf War. Sand-coloured flying suits did exist at the time, but Tornado squadrons were deployed before they were issued and so they went to war in NATO green. The Mk 31 and Mk 27 life preservers are unique to RAF Tornado crew. The Mk 31 has slight differences to previous issues such as the Mk 27. The Mk 31 makes use of a clip plate rather than buttons as seen in the Mk 27. The metal loop on the right sleeve connected to a strap from the ejection seat. During an ejection the strap would tighten to the wrists pinning the pilot in the seat. The beaded handle on the left-hand side of the life preserver on the Mk 27 version is used to inflate the stole once in the sea. The Mk 31 had a trumpet-shaped handle that was pulled down to inflate it.

The PEC shown was also specific to Tornados. When the aircraft was introduced, the newly upgraded electronics systems required an eight-pin connection known as a LEMO lead coming from the pilot's helmet. The PECs at the time still had NATO connectors, and an attachment was created for the transfer of LEMO to NATO between helmet and PEC. The Mk 4 flying helmet was introduced from the early 1980s. The shell of the helmet was a completely new design, but it retained the dual visor of the earlier flying helmets.

Our Parnavia Tornado pilot, wearing the kit initially used in the First Gulf War.

His life preserver is the Mk 27. There are two studs on the bottom of the life preserver, these allow connection of nuclear, biological and chemical warfare protection equipment if required. The upgrade to the Mk 31 was introduced shortly after the First Gulf War.

There are some notable differences for our Tornado pilot of the late 1990s/early 2000s, seen above. The bottom half of the uniform remains much the same, but the torso equipment is much improved with a more compact life preserver, designated a Mk 41. The large pouches seen by the waist are part of a separate survival waistcoat worn underneath the life preserver. They contained a variety of survival aids and were packed slightly differently depending on the theatre of operations. The 1965 pattern boots and white kid gloves remain a constant for aircrew.

The Blackburn (later Hawker Siddeley) Buccaneer was also on strength for the RAF in the early 1990s, although it was being phased out. It was a subsonic aircraft initially designed as a carrier-based aeroplane for the Royal Navy. It entered FAA service in 1962 and was initially rejected by the RAF, but when the BAC TSR2 project was cancelled and the purchase of the General Dynamics F-111K fell through, the RAF reluctantly accepted the Buccaneer. During the 1970s, the Royal Navy began a phased retirement of all its larger aircraft carriers, so from 1978 it was unable to effectively operate the Buccaneer, and any remaining airframes were passed on to the RAF.

Our post-First Gulf War Parnavia Tornado pilot.

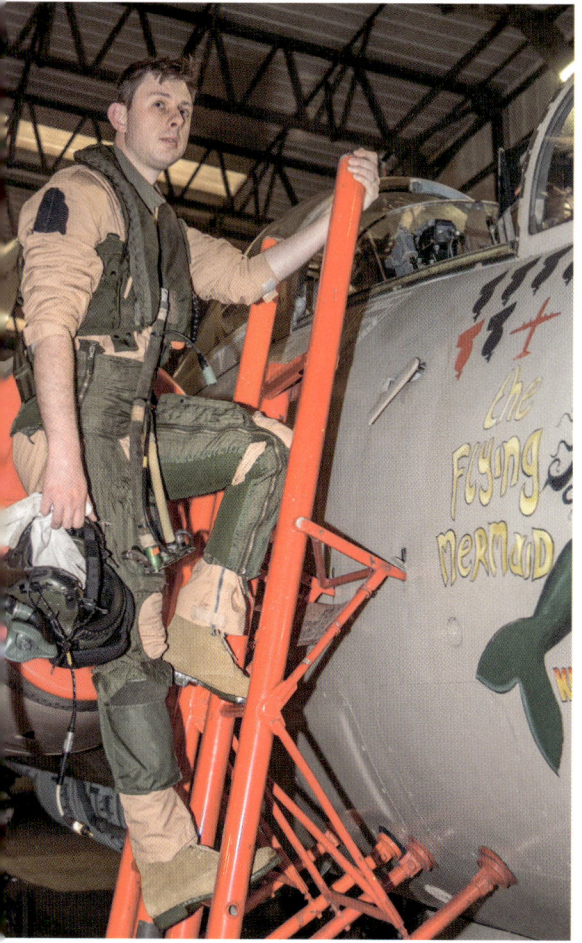

Above left: Our First Gulf War Buccaneer pilot climbs up to the cockpit of his desert-camouflaged aircraft, and is now wearing a desert camouflage flying suit.

Above right: Our First Gulf War Buccaneer pilot is now ready to take a flight, most likely for a guided bombing mission into enemy territory.

Pictured climbing into his desert painted Buccaneer, the pilot is wearing equipment for operation in the Gulf in 1991. Deploying later than Tornado squadrons, aircrew received the new desert-coloured flying suits and lightweight flying boots. Initially intended to help with targeting, the Buccaneer scored the only aerial combat victory by the RAF in the First Gulf War.

Like the life preserver of the Phantom pilot, but without the attached harness, his PEC clips directly to the front with two pins. Harnesses were eventually phased out with upgrades in ejection seat technology. The harness unlaced from inside the life preserver, and they were then redesignated to a Mk 22, which the pilot wears here. The PEC is an altered Royal Navy one with the under-water ejection cable removed and a blanking plate put over the attachment area for the air-ventilated suit. Over the suit he wears a pair of Mk 4 external anti-g trousers. In his right hand, he carries a Mk 4 flying helmet with oxygen mask and a pair of flying gloves.

Although the First Gulf War was brought to a fairly swift conclusion, the troubles in the Middle East would resurface, and the RAF would be called back for the Second Gulf War. The Buccaneers

Wearing standard equipment for a Harrier GR7 pilot flying over Kosovo in the late 1990s, our pilot wears anti-g trousers, two pairs of leg restraints, a survival vest and an Mk 30 life preserver.

Nearing the end of stand-down for Buccaneer crews in 1994, the two-man crew begin to enter the aircraft. Our pilots wear Mk 22 life preservers introduced just after the first Gulf War. The pilot at the top of the ladder wears a Mk 4 helmet.

were retired in 1994 while the Tornado continued to serve until 2019. The Tornado was one of the first modern multi-role aircraft capable of operating as a fighter, bomber, ground attack or reconnaissance platform, leading the way forward for the requirements of the RAF's latest aircraft.

Chapter 11

Contemporary RAF Pilots' Kit

In 2018, the RAF celebrated its 100th anniversary, having protected the skies over the United Kingdom and beyond for a century. Over this time, the role of the RAF expanded, and while it continues to protect British territories 24 hours a day, seven days a week, it has many other duties – most notably in the movement of essential equipment and supplies during the Covid pandemic. The RAF is also a key player in NATO and is constantly supporting allies all over the world in a range of humanitarian and military operations.

The RAF introduced the BAe Systems Hawk T1 in 1976 as its primary jet-training aircraft. The RAF Aerobatic Team, the Red Arrows, converted to this type in 1980. Despite its recent withdrawal (in favour of the Hawk T2) from most training squadrons, the Red Arrows still fly this aircraft today. The Red Arrows team is one of the best aerobatic teams in the world and represent the RAF at home and abroad. Each year, the team is made up of experienced pilots who have all flown front-line aircraft operationally.

A Eurofighter Typhoon taxis out for another training sortie at RAF Coningsby.

Above: Three modern-day Red Arrows pilots in full flying kit admiring the Hawk aircraft.

Below left: In training for a season of shows in the 1990s, a trainee Red Arrows pilot takes a breather after a training session in the sky.

Below right: Red Arrows pilots do not wear the famous red flying suits until they have completed training and achieved their Public Display Authority (PDA).

Wearing a Mk 14B flying suit, our pilot (on page 90) has the badge of the Red Arrows aerobatic team on his right arm. The Mk 14B didn't have any knee board pockets attached to the legs, denoting a fast-jet pilot who would be wearing anti-g trousers, who would have them as standard. His life preserver is a Mk 30, introduced in the early 1990s shortly after the First Gulf War. His helmet is a Mk 4.

His anti-g trousers are a pair of Mk 10s. These were designed to be a general issue with the hose from the internal bladder being able to protrude from either side of the trousers for use with different ejection seats. Note the holes on the right-hand side of the pilot. He also wears leg restraints and white flying gloves.

The image below right shows the Red Arrows kit as worn in the early 2000s. The equipment is on show at the RAF Museum Midlands and shows the standard kit for pilots on the team with the prestigious red flying suit. The helmet is a Mk 10, and there is a Mk 40L life preserver and Mk 4 external anti-g trousers.

The Eurofighter Typhoon is a multi-role aircraft that has been in use with the RAF since the early 2000s. It is currently the RAF's primary fighter aircraft, with several aircraft ready to scramble at any point on QRA protecting UK airspace. The Typhoon was developed by a consortium of European manufacturers consisting of Airbus, BAe Systems and Leonardo.

On page 93, this Typhoon pilot demonstrates the kit that was in use around 2008. Getting dressed for combat, this Typhoon pilot is at the beginning of the process with a liquid-cooled vest. Like the older

Above left: A close-up of our trainee showing a famous red-coloured pilots wing. Although not unique to the Red Arrows (some Tornado crews wore similar patches in the First Gulf War), they are not widely seen with all pilots.

Above right: A Red Arrows flying kit from the early 2000s, on display at the RAF Museum Midlands

Above left: Posing for the publicity cameras, a Typhoon pilot wears full kit as the aircraft banks overhead.

Above right: A liquid cooled vest, which would be covered by the flying suit.

air-cooled vests, it was found to be easier to control body temperature better and alter it more quickly with liquid. There are also a pair of liquid cooled socks!

Next, he wears a fleece inner suit for cool conditions after ejection. The smaller hole on the right-hand side of his waist is to take the tube of the vest. Over this, to make everything look respectable, is a desert version of the unique Typhoon flying suit. Also manufactured in green the flying suits were produced by Beaufort. There are two straight-zip pockets, a first aid dressing pocket on the right arm and pen pockets on the left. Rank is displayed on the epaulettes.

For flying, he wears a pair of full length trousers. Initially, this full cover version was only used on the Typhoon but has since seen service with the Red Arrows. On the top, he wears a life preserver with a similar system of restraint on ejection as a Tornado pilot. He has pockets for survival aids.

Almost complete, our pilot is wearing a Mk 4 flying helmet with Q-type mask. Mk 4s were gradually being phased out of service in favour of the Mk 10, but in early Typhoon squadron days, they could still be seen. He wears standard RAF boots and a pair of USAF Nomex gloves, which became common for pilots but were still worn alongside white, green and black RAF leather ones.

Today, the force continues to evolve and has recently taken delivery of its most advanced aircraft to date, the Lockheed Martin F35 Lightning II. The Lightning II will see a host of advances in a pilot's kit and equipment as personnel become more integrated into the aircraft and its technologies.

Above: Our Typhoon pilot getting ready for flight. Note his fleecy inner suit for cool conditions and the pattern of flying suit, which is unique to Typhoon pilots.

Right: Our Typhoon pilot heads out towards his aircraft. The kit has evolved considerably since the squadron's formation during World War Two.

RAF Kit Through the Ages

This is the civilian cotton and synthetic flight suit worn by BAE Systems test pilot Pete Cosogorin in 2015 when test flying the F35 Lightning II. It is currently on loan to the RAF Museum at Hendon.

The F35 Lightning II – the RAF's latest aircraft in the hands of a pilot from 617 Squadron 'The Dambusters'.

Summary

From 1900 to 1960, the world radically altered. In terms of aviation there was a quantum leap from no powered flight at the turn of that century to a supersonic aircraft streaking overhead. Technology has advanced so quickly, and, although this was great innovation, it was driven by great sacrifice. Two world wars drove aviation designers to overcome the challenges faced by aircrews to keep giving British pilots the cutting edge. Would the pace of change have been so rapid had it not been for global conflicts? It's hard to say. With the first jets flying in World War Two and evermore dangerous speeds being achieved, and manoeuvres being attempted, the safety of pilots was crucial – their lives and experiences were (and still are) vital to preserve.

The evolution of flying gear was inevitable as aircrew faced new threats, techniques and materials were discovered and created, making every innovation a little bit better every time. We owe a debt of gratitude to anyone who served and serves in the armed forces knowing that they may be asked to put their life on the line at any moment. Feeling safe and secure with the equipment you're given to do your job hopefully gives the confidence that's required to do it well.

Right: A flying helmet from World War One – a stark contrast to contemporary kit.

Below: The Mk 4 flying helmet with Q-type mask as used by Eurofighter Typhoon pilots, a far cry from the helmets used 100 years earlier.

Other books you might like:

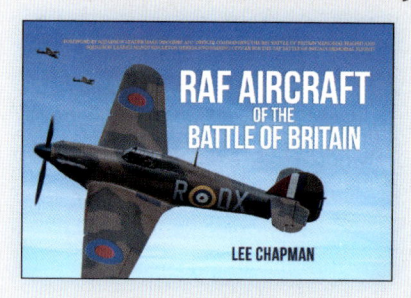

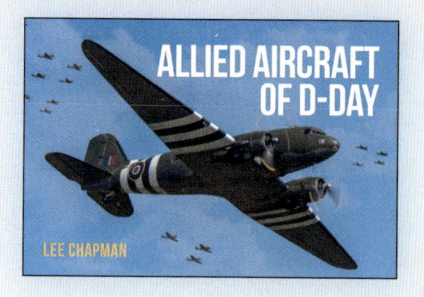

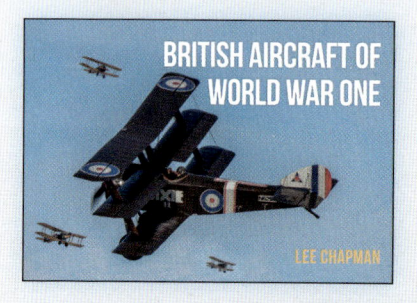

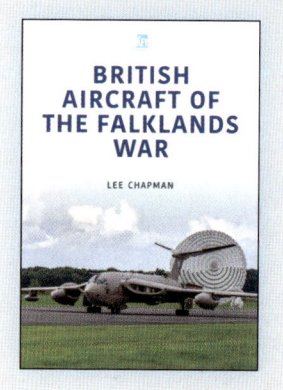

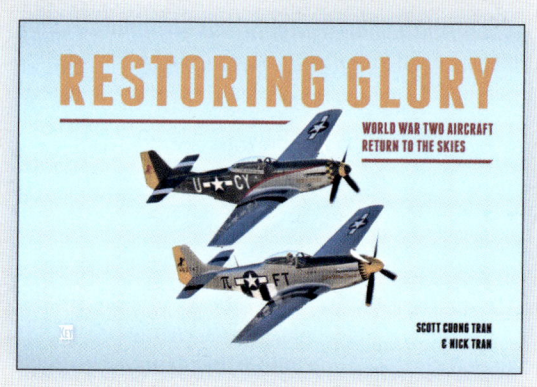

RAF Aircraft of the Battle of Britain — Lee Chapman

Allied Aircraft of D-Day — Lee Chapman

British Aircraft of World War One — Lee Chapman

British Interwar Aircraft — Lee Chapman

British Aircraft of the Falklands War — Lee Chapman

Restoring Glory: World War Two Aircraft Return to the Skies — Scott Cuong Tran & Nick Tran

For our full range of titles please visit:
shop.keypublishing.com/books

VIP Book Club

Sign up today and receive
TWO FREE E-BOOKS

Be the first to find out about our forthcoming book releases and receive exclusive offers.

Register now at **keypublishing.com/vip-book-club**

Our VIP Book Club is a 100% spam-free zone, and we will never share your email with anyone else. You can read our full privacy policy at: privacy.keypublishing.com